ROBERT
THE BRUCE

POCKET
GIANTS

D0492479

ROBERT THE BRUCE

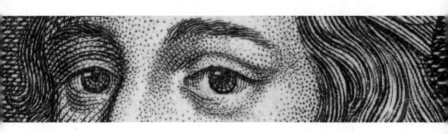

POCKET
GIANTS

FIONA
WATSON

Cover image © Mary Evans Picture Library

First published 2014

The History Press
The Mill, Brimscombe Port
Stroud, Gloucestershire, GL5 2QG
www.thehistorypress.co.uk

British Library Cataloguing in Publication Data.
A catalogue record for this book is available from the British Library.

ISBN 978 0 7524 9355 8

Typesetting and origination by The History Press
Printed in Malta by Gutenberg Press Ltd.

Contents

Introduction

Giant

Scots wha hae wi' Wallace bled,
Scots wham Bruce has oft-times led,
Welcome tae yer gory bed.
Or tae victory.

Robert Burns, 'Scots wha hae', 1793

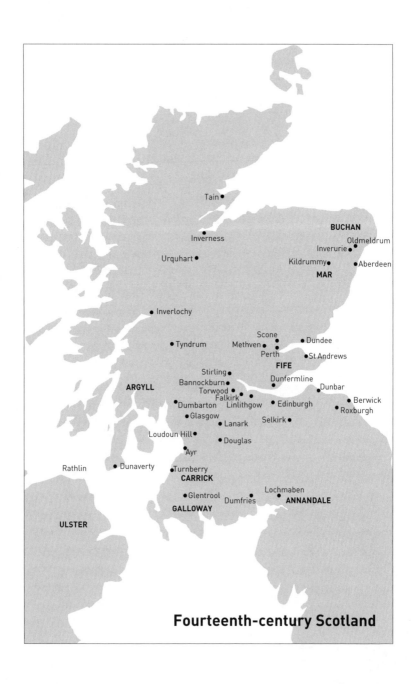

Tain •

BUCHAN

Inverness •

Oldmeldrum

Inverurie •

Urquhart •

Kildrummy •

• Aberdeen

MAR

• Inverlochy

Scone

• Tyndrum

Methven •

• Dundee

Perth

• St Andrews

FIFE

Stirling •

Bannockburn •

Dunfermline

Torwood •

• Dunbar

ARGYLL

Falkirk •

Linlithgow

Dumbarton •

• Edinburgh

• Berwick

• Glasgow

• Roxburgh

• Lanark

Selkirk •

Loudoun Hill •

• Douglas

Ayr •

Rathlin

• Dunaverty

• Turnberry

CARRICK

Lochmaben

• Glentrool

Dumfries

ANNANDALE

GALLOWAY

ULSTER

Fourteenth-century Scotland

Perched on a rocky summit high above a plain dotted with vineyards, the Castle of the Stars at Teba in Andalucía salutes the vastness of the azure sky. This is a dry land, drawn from a palate of browns and yellows and ochres. It is very different from Scotland, that wet, green place 1,800 miles away. And yet, on a late summer's day nearly 700 years ago, Scotland and Spain joined together on this very spot.

The memory of that moment lives on in Teba's small, neat square beneath the castle, where a giant slab of granite commemorates the help given by 'the Good' Sir James Douglas, formidable general and close friend of King Robert the Bruce, to Alfonso XI of Castile against the Moors, who still occupied much of Spain. Douglas had been entrusted with the task of taking his king's heart on pilgrimage to the Holy Land, a journey Bruce had always wanted to make in life but had never managed. Alas, Douglas and the Scots with him, in typically gung-ho fashion, charged so deep into enemy lines that they were cut off and most of them killed in the ensuing battle on 25 August 1330, though the castle was captured soon after. Both the body of Sir James and the casket containing Bruce's heart were brought home to Scotland. And so, after this final arduous journey, King Robert, who had died over a year earlier, was allowed to rest in peace, a legend both at home and abroad.

It was not always thus. Robert the Bruce was not born to be a giant. It is true that he inherited wealth, land and considerable privilege, but until the age of 32, his name is not one that should have drifted beyond the peaceful sanctuary of Scotland's more obscure history books, scarcely troubling the consciousness of present-day Scots, never mind inhabitants of the wider world. Bruce lived through extraordinary times, however, and these proved the perfect testing ground for his genius, forging a military leader with an international reputation for triumphing against the odds and putting his small, peripheral kingdom on the European map.

Much of what he did should make for uncomfortable reading. He was overwhelmingly ambitious, and ruthless with it – a fourteenth-century Macbeth in the eyes of some: a murderer, usurper and excommunicate. But he was also an extraordinarily innovative military commander who succeeded in liberating the medieval kingdom of Scotland from the control of its powerful southern neighbour, England. And he did so, to begin with at least, with the most limited of resources.

In 1314, at the Battle of Bannockburn, he defeated a numerically and – as contemporaries saw it – tactically superior cavalry army with a force made up almost entirely of foot soldiers armed with spears. His reign, partly as a result of the particular circumstances in which he took the throne, produced one of the most passionate and early expressions of the right of a nation to self-determination in medieval Europe. (Ironically, perhaps, the experience of fighting against Scotland also helped to crystallise and define England's identity and prompted her kings to remodel their armies, focusing also on the capability of the foot soldier – especially one armed with the longbow – which then served them so well during the Hundred Years War with France.) If Robert Bruce is less well known than other great military leaders, it is not because his deeds and reputation are less worthy, but because the theatre of war that he dominated has been undeservedly overlooked.

Today, Robert Bruce is regularly awarded the sobriquet of 'hero king' in Scotland. In 2006 he came third, with 12 per cent of the vote, in a list of 'most important Scots', behind William Wallace and Robert Burns.[1] His statues look down upon the people of Stirling, Edinburgh and Aberdeen, as well as presiding over the site of his great victory at Bannockburn (see Map). In his own day, he was known as 'The Bruce'[2] even by his enemies, a moniker that hints at affection among his own supporters and profound respect well beyond. 'The Bruce' was also the title given to the great epic poem written forty years after his death by Archdeacon John Barbour. Today he is most commonly referred to as Robert the Bruce.

However, a degree of ambivalence towards his reputation has developed over the last few centuries. Pursuit of his ambition to claim the throne of an independent Scotland is contrasted with the supposedly selfless and ideologically driven patriotism of William Wallace, another key figure in the Scottish wars with England. A strange form of class war has been projected on to these two heroes, with Wallace emerging as the champion of the working man, from whose forefathers he is deemed to spring, whilst Bruce is viewed as a member of a shifty, self-seeking nobility who espoused patriotism only when it was expedient to do so.

This version of their characters attained its most potent and wide-reaching form in the 1995 film *Braveheart.* Then the cult of Wallace, which had existed in Scotland for at least 500 years, reached a global audience. The film united two themes that struck a chord from Motherwell to Memphis to Medina: the desire to live freely and the ability of one man to change the world. 'Freedom', as it would have been understood in the thirteenth century, was a vastly different concept than it is today, rooted as it was in the social status of male property owners rather than the right of one nation or ethnic group to be responsible for its own destiny without interference from another. Equally, the myth of Wallace as a superman has long resided in his apparent responsibility for almost every blow struck in Scotland's struggle to rid herself of English rule during his lifetime, up to and including (in the film) fathering the next King of England after a brief liaison with the Princess of Wales. In reality, Wallace was one of a number of Scottish military commanders and, though he did become Guardian of Scotland[3] from the autumn of 1297 until his defeat at the Battle of Falkirk in July 1298, he later played a subsidiary role in the army of a subsequent Guardian. Even at his famous victory at Stirling Bridge in September 1297, he shared command with a young nobleman from northern Scotland, Andrew Murray.

Not even Hollywood dared to change Wallace's grisly demise, but at least the doomed hero could be portrayed showing Robert the Bruce the way, giving the film a 'happy ending' at Bannockburn, which, so it was implied, brought Scotland her freedom. This is certainly not a novel interpretation; almost from the beginning, histories of the wars written from a Scottish perspective have stressed what Bruce inherited from Wallace. But in reality, and despite the undeniably challenging fact that Bruce's ambitions brought him to fight his own people as much as the English, there is no comparison between the two men in terms of innovation, leadership and success. Wallace is the short-lived, ill-fated martyr. Bruce is the enduring, successful military genius – the monarch who, against the odds and the fallout of his own actions, forcibly united his kingdom and reigned for over two decades. A giant.

1

Origins

But Anthony Bek, bishop of Durham, put this
question to him [Edward I]:
   'If Robert of Bruce were king of Scotland, where
would Edward, king of England, be? For this Robert
is of the noblest stock of all England, and, with him,
the kingdom of Scotland is very strong in itself;
and, in times gone by, a great deal of mischief has
been wrought to the kings of England by those of
Scotland.'

John of Fordun,
Chronicle of the Scottish Nation, 1873

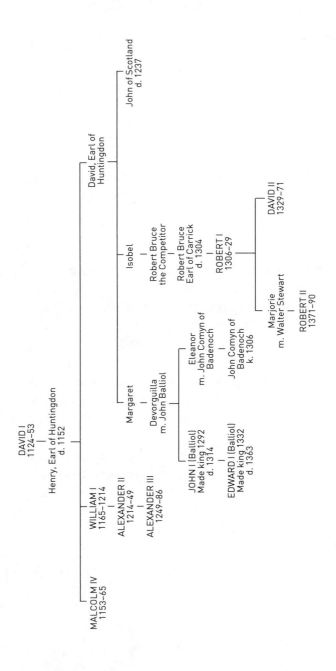

The Bruces, like many others, were an adventurous Norman family who exploited opportunities to increase their landed wealth and status in the British Isles in the decades following William of Normandy's conquest of England in 1066. Their original seat lay at Brix, near Cherbourg, but, by the early twelfth century, the first Robert Bruce had become Lord of Cleveland in North Yorkshire.

At some point after 1124, he was also granted the lordship of Annandale in south-west Scotland by the Scottish king, David I, who had grown up at the court of Henry I of England. Henry was married to David's elder sister, Matilda, and was the ultimate owner of the lands south of the River Forth. This territory had once been the most northerly part of Anglo-Saxon Northumbria but was formally granted to the Scottish kings, who already controlled it, in 975.

The civil war that broke out after King Henry's death in 1135 gave King David the excuse he needed to invade England, partly in defence of the claims of Henry's daughter, Matilda, against her cousin, Stephen of Blois, and partly in pursuit of more territory. For the last twenty years of his reign the Scottish king held the three northern

English counties of Cumberland, Westmorland and Northumberland. The gift of the lordship of Annandale with vice regal powers to Robert Bruce was not, therefore, about defending the border with England, which moved dramatically – if temporarily – some 100 miles further south during this period. Rather, it was intended that Bruce should keep an eye on the independent-minded lords of Galloway, west of Annandale, who had little enthusiasm for accepting the authority of the Scottish Crown.

Though they continued to hold lands in England, this branch of the Bruce family soon rooted itself firmly in Scotland, becoming well respected and well rewarded. The wife of the third Robert Bruce was an illegitimate daughter of the Scottish king, William I, while his nephew, the fourth Robert, married Isobel, a great-granddaughter of King David I, around 1219. It was this marriage that would provide Robert and Isabella's son – yet another Robert, nicknamed 'the Competitor' – with his claim to the throne of Scotland some seventy years later (see Family Tree).

In March 1286, the Scottish king, Alexander III, died riding through a storm to visit his new young queen. His three children by his first wife, Margaret, daughter of Henry III of England, had predeceased him. This left his granddaughter, a tiny Norwegian princess, as the only surviving direct heir. The Scottish nobility had already reluctantly promised to accept this Margaret as their future queen. However, Bruce the Competitor, now in his sixties, was adamant that he was a better choice as an adult male who, so he said, had been named heir to King Alexander II in the late 1230s, before the birth of the latter's son, the future Alexander III.

As Margaret's great-uncle and Scotland's nearest neighbour, King Edward I of England naturally took an interest in these events, not least in order to ensure that the dispute did not degenerate into civil war and destabilise his northern border. Relations between the two kingdoms had improved dramatically over the last few decades, once Scotland had officially given up on claims to the northern counties of England, and intermarriage and the wealth generated by their wool trade had encouraged many Scots to seek property south of the border.

The Scots were well aware that Edward could be high-handed and single-minded: the English king had run roughshod over native law and custom when he conquered Wales in the 1280s. Nevertheless, given the need to safeguard Margaret's future, the Scots were prepared to countenance her marriage to Edward's son, Prince Edward, with the safeguard of a treaty defending Scotland's integrity and independence.

However, the lynchpin of this agreement, the little princess herself, proved too delicate to survive the rigours of an autumnal crossing of the North Sea. She reached her father's island of Orkney at the end of September 1290 and died there, the sombre news then being carried to the Scottish nobility and English envoys waiting to greet her at Scone, near Perth. The Scots now faced the very real threat of a violent squabble over the throne between Bruce the Competitor and his neighbour in south-west Scotland,

John Balliol, Lord of Galloway, whose grandmother was the elder sister of Bruce's mother, Isobel (see Family Tree).

Deciding how a new king should be chosen, and by whom, was never going to be easy. However, whether the Scots liked it or not, King Edward, a renowned lawmaker, was determined to preside over the court that would make that decision. No doubt by now he also saw Scotland's vacant throne as an opportunity to extend his own power into the northern kingdom. Having encouraged other candidates to come forward and after making them all swear homage and fealty to him as Lord Superior of Scotland, King Edward's court took over a year to make its decision. Finally, in November 1292, it was adjudged that the rightful ruler of the northern kingdom was not the Competitor, but John Balliol. Despite later assertions to the contrary, most Scots agreed.

This first Scottish King John soon found himself caught between Edward of England's desire to turn his claims of lordship over the Scottish kingdom into specific obligations, and the desire of the Scots, led by Balliol's relatives, the powerful Comyn family (see Family Tree), to deny and resist this. In 1295, the Comyns found enough support to stage a palace revolution, taking control of government away from King John, whom they believed was unwilling to risk war with King Edward in defence of Scotland's independence. The next step was the conclusion of a treaty with England's great enemy, Philip IV of France. Although the Scots had allied with the French against the English before, most notably during the reign of Edward's grandfather, King John, this was the beginning of a longstanding alliance that, in theory at least, afforded both sides the protection of the other if attacked by England.

When Edward got wind of this he reacted furiously, though a man with a greater imagination would have recognised the extent to which the Scots had been pushed into the arms of the French by the English king's own actions. The following year he brought a huge army north, sacked the great border port of Berwick, sent the Earl of Surrey to defeat the Scots at Dunbar, formally divested Balliol of his kingship and set up his own direct government of Scotland.

The Bruces had joined with the English against King John, but were bitterly disappointed at Edward's quite unexpected resolve to keep the Scottish throne empty rather than award it to the Competitor's son.[4] Nevertheless, this Robert Bruce, the 6th Lord of Annandale, remained loyal to Edward I. But *his* son, the Earl of Carrick, joined resistance to English rule, which began to erupt spontaneously in various parts of Scotland from the late spring of 1297. For the seventh Robert Bruce, it was the beginning of a long and brutal contest that would ultimately be played for the highest of stakes.

2

The Testing Ground (1297–1306)

Hardly had a period of six months passed since the Scots had bound themselves by the above-mentioned solemn oath of fidelity and subjection to the king of the English, when the reviving malice of that perfidious [race] excited their minds to fresh sedition.

Chronicle of Lanercost, 1913

This youngest Robert Bruce – grandson of the Competitor and the future king – was born in 1274. Astonishingly, given that an epic poem thousands of lines long was written about him only some forty years after his death, we have nothing on which to base a description. A forensic reconstruction of what was long believed to be his skull, moulded from the original in the nineteenth century when a tomb in Dunfermline Abbey was temporarily reopened, presents us with a pudgy, square-faced man sporting what can only be described as a cauliflower nose. Unfortunately, doubt has recently been cast on whether this is actually King Robert, with academic opinion now favouring his great-great-great-great-grandfather, King David I.

In the dark days of November 1292, when it was no secret that John Balliol was about to be proclaimed as the rightful King of Scots, Bruce the Competitor proposed a series of extraordinary dynastic somersaults to his progeny. He knew that he was too old to fight this battle another day. So he charged his son – Earl of Carrick[5] through his marriage to the heiress, Marjory – with taking the family's claim to the throne forward in whatever way he could.

To that end, it was imperative that this middle Robert Bruce should hold no land in Scotland requiring him to swear homage and fealty – a solemn and binding oath – to the new Balliol king. The Competitor retained his vast lordship of Annandale, but Carrick was now passed on to his grandson, 18-year-old Robert, who became an earl. Shortly thereafter, the latter married Isobel, daughter of Donald, Earl of Mar – a close ally of his grandfather. Though Isobel was dead by 1297, the couple had a daughter, named Marjory after Carrick's mother.

Around the same time, the young earl decided to try a different tack, rather than hoping, like his father, that loyalty to Edward I would help them to fulfil their ambitions. What Carrick was taking astute advantage of was the fact that most of the Comyns – Scotland's most powerful political family – had been imprisoned or forced into exile in England for their part in fighting against Edward on Balliol's behalf in 1296.

This was a power vacuum that young Carrick now tried to exploit. In the early summer of 1297, he, along with his friend and neighbouring lord, James the Steward, and the powerful Bishop of Glasgow, Robert Wishart, called out their armies in protest at King Edward's demands that 'the middling sort' of Scotland should fight with him in his impending campaign against France. This was viewed as an outrageous and potentially debilitating imposition on men who, though not nationally prominent, were nonetheless important leaders in their own communities. At the same time,

Carrick and his allies were positioning themselves as the voice of Scotland's political community.

The timing was well planned too, coming as it did not long after William Wallace launched the first known attack on English officials at Lanark, south-east of Glasgow, on 3 May 1297. Initially, the Scots were only loosely co-ordinated. However, the prospect of a group of senior noblemen joining the unrest seriously alarmed the English government based in Berwick and an army sent out against them spent most of June negotiating their surrender. As part of that agreement, Carrick and the others were supposed to hand over hostages: in the earl's case, his baby daughter. Over the coming months, considerable pressure – including the ravaging of his father's lordship of Annandale (inherited in 1295) – was put upon the earl to comply, but he never gave Marjory up.

Despite this aristocratic capitulation, Andrew Murray and William Wallace were still attacking English garrisons and Edward was sufficiently concerned to countenance the release of members of the Comyn family explicitly to deal with them. The latter, like many of the Scottish nobility, sat on the fence until the Scottish victory at Stirling Bridge against the Earl of Surrey in September 1297. With almost all English garrisons expelled from the country, it made sense to revive the position of Guardian to run those parts of Scotland not under English control until King John was able to return from imprisonment in England. With Andrew Murray dead from his wounds, William Wallace was the obvious candidate to hold the office, despite not coming from a noble family. He earned himself a knighthood at the same time, reputedly – though there is no evidence for it – at the hands of Robert Bruce, Earl of Carrick. Ten months later, however, Sir William was defeated by King Edward at Falkirk and, since success in warfare was the sole reason for his elevation, he was forced to resign as Guardian. By the end of 1298, Sir John Comyn, the younger, of Badenoch – King John's nephew – and Robert Bruce, Earl of Carrick, had become joint Guardians in an uneasy compromise between these two powerful families.

It did not take long for the two young men to come to blows as both sought to take advantage of the possibilities afforded by an absent king. The year 1299 was comparatively quiet, since Edward was focused on his marriage to Philip of France's sister, Marguerite, rather than a campaign in Scotland. In August, Scotland's leaders, including the two Guardians, dared to meet in Selkirk Forest, in the heart of English-held territory. An altercation began between one of Comyn's men and Sir Malcolm Wallace – the former Guardian's elder brother, who was part of Carrick's retinue – because Sir William was known to be going to the Continent to lobby for support on behalf of King John without Sir John Comyn's permission.

Word of the scuffle reached Comyn and he immediately seized Carrick by the throat, crying treason, while his cousin, the Earl of Buchan, rounded on the Bishop of St Andrews, William Lamberton. Cooler heads stepped in to calm things down and, in light of news of a raid by pro-English Scots in the north that needed their immediate attention, it was agreed that Lamberton should become a third, and chief, Guardian, to keep the peace between the other two.

In the summer of 1299, Pope Boniface VIII forced King Edward to release King John into papal custody. Sir William Wallace's embassy to the courts of Europe was a direct result. Over the following months, the Scots marshalled their arguments and sent highly eloquent churchmen to Rome to persuade Boniface to demand that Edward justify his take-over of Balliol's kingdom. They also hoped that the pope would intervene personally and judge the whole issue of Scotland's status vis-à-vis England himself, gambling that this would be in their favour. The Scots were useful to both Boniface and Philip of France, each of whom then had their own disputes with King Edward, and they made the most of their opportunity.

The Earl of Carrick had done well to stay in power for so long, but ultimately he proved no match for his powerful rivals. By May 1300, he had been ousted as joint Guardian and resolved to remain quietly on his estates in western Scotland, hedging his bets by fighting for neither side. The English king continued to bring armies north to extend his grip south of the Rivers Forth and Clyde. After losing at Falkirk, the Scots wisely decided not to fight any more pitched battles, preferring instead to harry English supply lines and attack their garrisons once Edward's armies had returned home for the winter. However, despite some

Scottish success in this guerrilla warfare, there is no doubt that the English king was slowly but surely winning the war on the ground.

The same could not be said of the war of words on the Continent. At some point in 1301, Philip IV of France changed the rules of the diplomatic game once again by acquiring custody of King John, with or without Pope Boniface's permission. By the end of that year, even Edward had to admit that the Scottish king might soon be returning home at the head of a French army.

This was too much for the Earl of Carrick. Not only had his father's castle of Lochmaben been occupied by English forces since 1298 (presumably because of its strategic importance and with the excuse of Carrick's rebellion, despite Bruce senior's steadfast adherence to Edward), but he also lost control of his own earldom to the English king during the campaign of 1301. Then, to make matters worse, a truce was agreed between England and Scotland in January 1302 under France's auspices. By its terms, Edward was obliged to hand over any lands recently captured, including Carrick, to King Philip on behalf of King John. Early in 1302, as King Edward retreated dismally from Scotland, his army starving and disease-stricken, the earl – aged 28 – came to his peace.

Carrick certainly had his uses to the English king. If Balliol was on the verge of coming home, it would do no harm to try to split the Scots by implying that the Bruces' alternative 'right' to the throne – under Edward's overlordship, of course – might now be resurrected. As a reward, the earl was given the English king's goddaughter, Elizabeth de Burgh, in marriage. Her father's earldom of Ulster was only a short boat journey across the Irish Sea from Carrick, whose own earls had previously held lands and some influence in the north of Ireland. Lochmaben remained in Edward's hands, presumably until Carrick proved trustworthy.

As it turned out, the tide of good fortune on which the hopes of King John and his supporters had been raised receded even more quickly. Their successes, though fiercely lobbied for in the courts of Europe, relied on the strategic needs of others, and in 1302, for very different reasons, both King Philip and Pope Boniface needed to befriend Edward I. Balliol realised that the game was over, for him at least, and resigned his claim to the throne of Scotland to his French protector. Although John Comyn of Badenoch and many other Scots resolved to fight on, they had considerably less ability to resist Edward now that they had been sent into the diplomatic cold. Carrick may have felt that he had jumped too soon, but at least he had a head start with King Edward when, at the beginning of 1304, Comyn, now sole Guardian, led the rest of the Scots to submit en masse.

Carrick was a major player in the final phases of this, Edward's second conquest of Scotland. He acted as Sheriff of Lanark and Ayr and rode with a small cohort of trusted knights to look for those Scots, like Sir William Wallace, recently returned from the Continent, who continued to resist. It was the price of submission that they should hunt down Wallace, on whom Edward now heaped his wrath for the terrible deaths of so many of his people and the destruction of land and property in large swathes of northern England.

On 21 April 1304, during the final phase of the reconquest, Carrick's father died. At 30 years old, the seventh Robert Bruce inherited not only his family's great lordship of Annandale and the castle of Lochmaben (which Edward now had no reason to keep from him), but also the claim to the throne. Within only a few weeks, he was already trying to reawaken this dormant ambition.

As King Edward's great army sat around to watch the engineers bring the last castle held in the name of King John to its knees – Stirling, which commands the vital crossing point of the River Forth in the very heart of Scotland – Carrick made an agreement with William Lamberton, Bishop of St Andrews. It was deliberately vague: a promise of mutual aid in unspecified circumstances; but nowhere did either man mention his allegiance to the English king. They were looking to a future in which this would no longer be a consideration.

At the same time, Edward no longer had the same need for Carrick as he did in 1302, while he was equally well aware that he had to work with the Comyn family; their power and influence made it hard to govern Scotland without their support, as he had discovered in 1297. By the end of 1305, the English king had enjoyed the satisfaction of Wallace's capture and brutal execution, and had put the finishing touches to how Scotland was to be governed. Though Sir John Comyn of Badenoch, who had been Guardian for much of the period between 1298 and 1304, was not given an official role, many of his friends and relatives were. His cousin, the Earl of Buchan, and his right-hand man, Sir John Moubray, were both members of a council to advise the new Royal Lieutenant in Scotland, Edward's nephew, John of Brittany.

Carrick was also on the council, but must have felt that little had changed since the days when, as joint Guardian, he had tried and failed to share power with the Comyns. To add insult to injury, an inquiry had been ordered into the vice regal rights that the lords of Annandale had long enjoyed on their estates – the kind of power that Edward viewed as excessive for a nobleman.

The king never pronounced on this thorny issue. At the beginning of 1306, nearly ten years after the original invasion, Edward I was 66 years old and in failing health. Carrick knew this and was already making preparations, hoarding provisions in several castles along the west coast. We should not doubt that he intended to make a bid for the throne once Edward was dead and the Scots had been liberated from their oaths of allegiance. But if Carrick envisioned a straightforward path to the empty throne of Scotland, it was soon obscured by an almost insurmountable obstacle.

3

The Trouble with Robert the Bruce

Now this Robert the Bruce was a remarkably brave and strong man: there was no man in Scotland that was thought a match for him except Sir William Wallace; and now that Wallace was dead, Bruce was held the best warrior in Scotland ... He was generous, too, and courteous by nature; but he had some faults, which perhaps belonged as much to the fierce period in which he lived as to his own character.

W. Scott,
Tales of a Grandfather, 1869

For those still interested in resurrecting Scotland's ancient kingship, the issue had become considerably more complicated than it was in the early 1290s, when the essential choice had been between Bruce the Competitor and John Balliol. Carrick certainly had no intention of letting go of the argument that it was necessary to go back to Alexander III and re-establish that the next in line to the throne, now that Balliol was out of the picture, was a Bruce.

However, this was not the only argument as to who should be king in 1306. Nor was it necessarily the most credible. Despite the fact that John Balliol had been forced to abdicate by Edward I in 1296 (and had even renounced his rights to the Scottish throne in favour of Philip of France when the diplomatic tables turned in 1302), he was still the last King of Scots to have been duly and properly inaugurated. Any future king should therefore be one of his descendants. Alexander III was, according to this line of thinking, irrelevant.

At a practical level it could also be argued that Balliol's son, Edward (born *c.* 1282), was now the heir, but unfortunately he was still in custody in England. However, King John's nephew was very much at liberty and living in Scotland, a man of pre-eminent power and influence

– Sir John Comyn of Badenoch. We will probably never know the reason for the meeting between Sir John and the Earl of Carrick on 10 February 1306 in the church of the Greyfriars of Dumfries in south-west Scotland, so coloured is it by subsequent events. However, we do know that Badenoch was murdered, along with his uncle, Sir Robert, near the high altar.

English sources are generally agreed, with hindsight, that Carrick plotted Badenoch's removal in order to clear his own way to the throne, while later Scottish sources accuse Sir John of having betrayed to Edward I an agreement between himself and Carrick as to which of them should be king. The truth is probably less calculating and more mundane – a meeting called ostensibly to discuss a dispute between them as local landowners (Badenoch held Dalswinton, 7 miles north of Dumfries) in the wake of a justiciary court held earlier that day, which probably degenerated when the subject turned to what might happen in Scotland once Edward I was dead. Bruce and his friends were wearing armour, symptomatic either of premeditation or insecurity. Comyn was not dressed so – a testament perhaps to his personal confidence, his position in Scottish society and the fact that noblemen generally do not stab each other. On the other hand, the two had certainly never got on, primarily because they wanted the same thing, and this showdown was the final act after years of tension between them.

Carrick was immediately stricken by the enormity of what he had done. He appealed to Edward I, via his officials in Berwick, to protect him from the dead man's family. However, he soon realised that he had no choice but to take the advice of the ancient yet still influential Bishop of Glasgow, Robert Wishart, and seize the throne without delay. It was what he had planned, but it was certainly not the way he had planned it.

With the benefit of hindsight, however, there can be little doubt that if Carrick wished to make good on his claim to the throne, then he would inevitably have had to deal with the Comyns by force; they would never have accepted him as king because their own political power would have been eclipsed as a result. Equally, it turned out that Robert the Bruce was by far and away the best man to restore an independent Scotland. Nevertheless, this was certainly not obvious to contemporaries.

The crucial problem, apart from the Comyns, was Edward I himself, ailing but still very much alive. Leaving aside the sacrilegious murder, Carrick faced an uphill struggle to persuade most Scottish nobles to break their solemn oaths of homage and fealty to the English king, sworn so recently and voluntarily, even if they could envisage the need to find an active, vigorous king for Scotland once Edward was dead. Nevertheless, on 25 March 1306, six weeks after Comyn's murder, Robert Bruce, Earl of Carrick was made King of Scots at Scone near Perth, the traditional site of royal inaugurations.

Such a ceremony should have been both exalted and magnificent, one of the most important opportunities to emphasise the unity of the kingdom under its ancient line of kings. In 1249, when Alexander III was crowned, the Earls of Fife and Strathearn led him from the Augustinian abbey of Scone to a cross in its graveyard. There a throne had been prepared, 'decked with silken cloths inwoven with gold', where he sat while the Bishop of St Andrews and others consecrated him as king 'as was meet'. Finally, a poet had stepped forward to recite, in Gaelic, the names of the new monarch's ancestors, going back to Fergus – supposedly the first King of Scots – and then further still, to the very progenitor of his race: reputedly Iber Scot, whose father was a Prince of Greece and whose mother was a pharaoh's daughter.[6]

Not surprisingly, given the dramatic events that preceded the ceremony and the fact that Edward I had made off in 1296 with the Stone of Scone, which traditionally sat beneath the throne at inaugurations, Bruce's crowning was rather makeshift and badly attended. Bishop Wishart was certainly present, adding a degree of pomp and convention to proceedings by digging out 'robes and vestments suitable for a new king to wear, and also a banner bearing the arms of the last king, which the indefatigable old man had been carefully hiding in his treasury for precisely this purpose and moment'.[7] He was joined by the Bishop of Moray and two abbots.

Scotland's most senior prelate, William Lamberton of St Andrews, stayed away initially, presumably out of fear or conscience or both, but was then 'persuaded' to come and say Mass. The Earls of Atholl and possibly Menteith and Lennox were present – a poor showing out of a total of eleven of that rank (excluding Carrick himself). Isobel, Countess of Buchan and wife of the murdered Badenoch's cousin, came to perform her family's pivotal role in making Scottish kings on behalf of her nephew, the Earl of Fife. Nevertheless, it was scarcely a resounding start to King Robert's reign, and many must have wondered just how long he would survive.

Of those who had lands to lose for supporting Bruce in these early days, we can count fewer than 200.[8] Some, like James Douglas, had been deprived of property and position during the previous phase of the war and calculated that they had much to gain by switching allegiance; some had personal connections to the new king; and others no doubt believed that it was worth overlooking the terrible events that had precipitated Bruce's seizure of the throne for Scotland's greater good. None of them had any idea how successful he might become. They were gambling, just like their new king, on a series of imponderables. How long would Edward I live? How well would his son, Edward II, manage Scottish affairs? What kind of an opposition would the Comyns and their allies muster? Above all, what sort of a leader would Robert Bruce turn out to be? Given his career so far, they had very little to go on.

In taking the throne in such a messy, unlawful way, Bruce changed the course of Scottish history. For now the writers and chroniclers – almost exclusively churchmen – needed to find the words to show that this extraordinary turn of events was exactly what God had planned all along. They had a number of targets for their propaganda: Edward I and his 'illegal' conquest of Scotland, an argument already articulated during the previous phase of the war; John Balliol's inferior claim to the Scottish throne, an idea that ran not just contrary to reality but also to what the Scots had previously argued; and John Comyn's treachery towards Bruce, which would serve to justify his murder, and the subsequent horrific treatment of parts of Scotland previously under his family's sway.

Much of what has been written about the life of Robert the Bruce is based on a great romance poem written in the 1370s by the Archdeacon of Aberdeen, John Barbour. *The Bruce* purports to tell the truth about what happened. In fact, it is a highly partial account, the purpose of which was to put a chivalric gloss on the king's brutal struggle against his many enemies. Written in the style of the great French *romans-histoires*, it quickly became *the* authorised version of events, meaning that there was no need for later medieval Scottish historians to go into too much detail about the period. They simply assumed that everyone reading or listening to their histories knew the poem and hurried on, except where they wished to make specific points or emphasise particular themes. It certainly did not occur to them to mount any serious challenge to Barbour, although occasionally snippets of older material written before 1306, when it was not de rigueur to bolster the reputation of Robert the Bruce, were sometimes thrown in to hint at an alternative point of view.[9]

As a result, it has taken the best part of 700 years for many of the myths surrounding the life and times of King Robert to be challenged – an example of successful 'spin' that would leave modern political apologists gasping with envy. The reputations of Sir John Comyn and his family have been blackened to the point where even the most authoritative recent biographer of King Robert can assert that the man who led the Scots throughout most of the first phase of the war was 'an almost total failure'.[10]

Even more widespread is a profoundly negative perception of John Balliol, whose throne Bruce seized. This has largely arisen from the deliberate misinformation concocted by those writing after 1306 that the former was chosen as king in 1292 because he was deemed the most pliant by Edward I, contrary to the wishes of the Scots. Although King John will never emerge from the record as a particularly forceful personality, his claim was generally regarded as the best at the time, and it was Bruce the Competitor – not Balliol – who showed himself most willing to agree to whatever King Edward wanted during the competition for the throne.

Working out how best to present Robert's kingship as a legitimate extension of the long line of monarchs stretching back into antiquity – itself a reflection of the ancient independence of the kingdom – exercised the minds of many of the historians of Scotland who came after Barbour, just as it had taxed the ingenuity of Bruce's own writers of history. It was seen as essential to close ranks on this issue, whatever the truth of the matter, for to do otherwise might give credence to the terrible spectre of English overlordship.

Ironically, given that King Robert was as much of a usurper as men like Henry IV and Richard III of England, later Scottish historians like John of Fordun came down hard on previous kings who were deemed to have stolen the Crown from legitimate heirs. One stands out in this regard: an eleventh-century ruler of great renown at the time found himself stigmatised for a series of crimes against the line of Kenneth MacAlpin – allegedly (though not actually) the first to rule over the kingdom of Alba and the progenitor of the royal family from whom Bruce claimed descent. This king's name was Macbeth.[11]

Digging into such well-entrenched myths in a systematic and meaningful way has only just begun, thanks to the growing sophistication and confidence of those now engaged in writing Scottish history. The task is a delicate one. Of course, we must establish a more nuanced and objective version of events, but equally we must be careful not to become overly cynical or detached. The wars with England produced much propaganda on all sides, especially on behalf of King Robert. Some of it is impassioned and beautiful – a testament to the scholarship and expressive capabilities of Scotland's churchmen. That they should have played fast and loose with some of the more inconvenient truths must be exposed and discussed.

But equally we must acknowledge the possibility that, for them, there was a 'greater truth', or at least a bigger picture, which made it imperative that they overlook certain elements of the story or retell it in a particular light. For those living in difficult times there are often no 'right' answers and many will suffer no matter what course of action is decided upon.

The views of those who felt passionately that what Bruce had done could never be justified must be heard too. We have come to recognise their voices occasionally embedded within the works of later historians, who quite happily plagiarised material from earlier sources. We can now reach back to a time when the writers of history were more likely to praise the name of Comyn than Bruce. They may have been gilding the lily just as much as Barbour et al., but in recognising their very different political perspective, we are forcibly reminded that there was nothing inevitable about King Robert's rise to power and the remarkable military achievements that were the real reason for keeping him there.

4

A King in Search of his Throne (1306–09)

And when King Edward was told
How the Bruce that was so bold,
Had finished off the Comyn
And how he since then had been made king,
He nearly went out of his mind.

John Barbour,
The Bruce, 2007

The first year of Robert I's reign was nothing short of a complete disaster. The new king was exposed as an incompetent warrior with neither the experience nor the ability to impose himself successfully on Edward's forces, or those loyal to the Comyn family and the former king, John Balliol. Bruce's young queen, Elizabeth de Burgh, summed up the situation rather well when she allegedly commented to her husband, shortly after they were inaugurated at Scone, that she was afraid they were merely playing at being king and queen 'like children'.[12]

King Edward was at first fairly sanguine about the murder in Dumfries, regarding it as an internal issue of law and order that could be dealt with by his officials in the north. But it was a completely different matter once he heard that there was a new king in Scotland. Now John Comyn was seen as a martyr to Bruce's ambitions and on 5 April 1306, the very day he was told about the inauguration, Edward grimly appointed his cousin, Sir Aymer de Valence, to organise the crushing of this shocking new rebellion, ordering him 'to burn and slay and raise the dragon';[13] in other words, to give no quarter.

De Valence caught up with Bruce at Methven, 7 miles west of Perth in east central Scotland, on 19 June. The new king and his men were clearly rattled by the thought that none of them, no matter how illustrious, would find mercy should they be captured; they had taken the precaution of covering their armour – which bore their individual coats of arms – with white shirts, so that they could not be identified. The Scottish king was still confident, or naïve, enough to consider taking on his enemies in battle – something the Scots had given up, for good reason, after the rout at Falkirk eight years earlier.

It was de Valence who adopted the more cunning and creative approach, the English also having learned that the chivalric rulebook was not terribly useful when fighting in the boggy uplands of Scotland. Protesting that they would not give battle on a feast day – a story the Scottish king was foolish to believe – English forces caught Bruce's men off guard and preparing to eat. The result was not in doubt. Many Scots were captured and King Robert himself only just managed to avoid being taken.

Bruce had little choice but to flee west, where he felt most at home, only to find his way blocked near Tyndrum by the forces of John Macdougall of Lorne, a cousin of the slain Comyn. Once again he was defeated, and what remained of his army began to disintegrate. He was now on the run in his own kingdom with only his closest friends and family in support. Sending his womenfolk north under the care of his brother, Neil, Bruce headed even further west, to his castle of Dunaverty on the southernmost tip of the peninsula of Kintyre. His enemies were only just behind him.

Acutely aware of the danger he was in, like Bonnie Prince Charlie four centuries later, he escaped by boat across the Irish Sea. He made first for the small island of Rathlin off the north coast of Antrim, where, as Earl of Carrick, he may still have had connections. From there, Bruce most probably moved north to the Hebrides and the lands of the Lady of Garmoran, Christina Macruari, in whose care he spent the winter of 1306–07. His enemies called him 'King Hobbe', a name that was not only the diminutive of Robert, but had connotations of evil and annoyance.[14]

He was extraordinarily lucky not to be captured and executed. His younger brothers Thomas and Alexander suffered hanging, drawing and quartering after they were caught as part of an expeditionary force sent to Galloway in February 1307. Neil Bruce likewise suffered the ultimate penalty for his brother's ambitions. He and the Earl of Atholl had taken the queen, his sisters Christian and Mary Bruce, King Robert's daughter Marjory (now aged about 10) and Isobel, Countess of Buchan, who had crowned the king, to Kildrummy Castle in Mar as Bruce fled west after Methven. After a fire was started deliberately within the castle, the royal party fled further north. They were probably hoping to reach Norway, where another Bruce sister, Isobel, was queen dowager, but were captured by the Earl of Ross at the shrine of St Duthac's at Tain, north of Inverness. The women were imprisoned – Isobel of Buchan and Mary Bruce in cages hung from two Scottish castles – and the men put to death.

For Robert, this was not only a bitter personal blow; it stymied any prospect of a direct male heir, the very issue that had precipitated the wars between Scotland and England in the first place. Only his last surviving brother, Edward, stood between the Bruces and short-lived possession of the Crown of Scotland.

This was the low point of King Robert's life and career. He had only himself to blame for the onset of these dark days, which were a product of unwavering ambition, a rush of blood to the head in Dumfries and failure to think of ways to deal effectively with his many enemies. There is no doubt that Bruce could tap into a deep-seated desire on the part of many Scots to be rid of what they now regarded as foreign occupation and aggression. But this was of little use if he could not survive in, let alone make a success of, his new role as warrior king.

It was in this very abyss, however, that Bruce found his strength and his genius. The legend of the spider in the cave that persuaded him to try, try and try again dates from much later and was first told about James Douglas, Bruce's friend and general, rather than the king himself. Yet the example of this tenacious arachnid serves as well as any other explanation for the subsequent transformation in his military thinking, and therefore his fortunes, since there is nothing in our sources to which we can attribute its cause. Perhaps Bruce took part in warfare in Ireland or western Scotland over that winter on behalf of whoever was protecting him? Perhaps he picked up some tips on using the element of surprise and travelling lightly over difficult terrain? Or did he study his own nation's previous military history with its emphasis on fast-moving raids across the border into England and a general aversion for pitched battles and taking castles, combined with the lessons of recent successes in European history for infantry prepared to use natural features to mitigate the natural superiority of cavalry? We have no way of knowing. But he certainly seems to have thought out a blueprint for success during the short days and long nights of his exile.

Bruce's return to his homeland in February 1307 nearly ended in yet another disaster. The target was his own castle of Turnberry in Carrick, which perches on a rocky outcrop surrounded on three sides by the sea, looking out beyond the domed island of Ailsa Craig towards Ulster. The scout who had been sent on ahead judged that it was too heavily defended, but was caught out when someone else lit a bonfire, the signal that it was safe for the king to come ashore. Bruce, however, decided to carry on, ignoring the castle and killing those Englishmen billeted in the undefended village instead. Now, using the element of surprise, he and his men made the glens and moorlands of Carrick and neighbouring Galloway their base, sweeping down into the valleys to demand supplies from the fearful locals – less time-consuming than the hunting and berry picking to which they had previously been reduced – causing havoc and mayhem among English garrisons, and at the same time gathering men to him.

The king may have been on the run still, and always wary of being betrayed, but at least he was on home soil and his confidence was returning. In April 1307, Bruce finally won his first victory, trapping English forces in the narrow, wooded confines of Glentrool in Galloway, killing a number of enemy soldiers and sending the rest fleeing.

The main English army under de Valence was further north, at Ayr. At last Bruce felt strong enough to take him on again. At Loudoun Hill, 23 miles from de Valence's base, he prepared his forces on high and exposed moorland guarding the road east. He would not be caught out by a ruse this time; nor would he allow the English cavalry to overwhelm his spearmen, as they would normally expect to do. Instead he sought to restrict the movements of de Valence's horsemen by digging trenches at right angles to the road. These would allow only a small number of cavalry to pass through and at the same time protect his own men from attack from the side and rear. On the day of the battle – *c.* 10 May 1307 – the King of Scots himself fought at the front of his 600 men with his only surviving brother, Edward, at his side.

The strategy worked. The first wave of enemy cavalry baulked at riding on to Scottish spears. The Scots – who already seem by this stage to be well trained and highly disciplined – pushed them back, causing those behind to panic and retreat. Barbour's account of the battle raises parallels with Bruce's most famous victory at Bannockburn, where ditches or pits were also dug and Scottish spearmen proved equally adept at pushing the horsemen on to their comrades behind.[15]

Though small in scale, the significance of the victory at Loudoun Hill was immense. It proved that, even if Bruce had been excommunicated by the pope for the murder of John Comyn, God could still favour him. This must have been a great relief to 18-year-old James Douglas, who had just joined King Robert after much indecision, having failed to recover his family lands from Edward I. Douglas was not apparently renowned for his beauty, being 'somewhat pale, and, as I [John Barbour] heard it, he had black hair'. He also had a lisp like Hector of Troy and, indeed, Edward I, which in those days was regarded as a manly attribute.[16] He was strong and well made, and would ultimately prove to be one of King Robert's greatest generals.

Loudoun Hill also added to the short list of battles won by foot soldiers against cavalry in this period, the most impressive of which had been at Courtrai in Flanders in 1302. Here the streams and ditches of the battlefield had prevented the French cavalry army from being able to charge the Flemish townsmen properly. It is quite possible that Bruce had turned to reports of this miraculous victory and learned what he could from it.

Edward I was both astonished and incensed that 'King Hobbe' was not only still on the loose, but capable of besting an English force. The ailing English king decided to come north on campaign himself. But, on 7 July 1307, he died at Burgh-on-Sands near Carlisle, having failed to cross the border. His son, Edward II, rushed north and marched into south-western Scotland after Bruce, but the

Scottish king kept his distance and, after a few months, Edward returned south to organise his coronation.

Bruce could now turn his attention to his enemies within Scotland. As the autumn of 1307 succumbed to the sharp grip of winter he rampaged across the north. But such hyperactivity took its toll after the privations of his time on the run and rumours abounded that the king was gravely ill. Such stories proved extremely premature, however: in May the following year, he defeated John Comyn's cousin, the Earl of Buchan, on the road between Inverurie and Oldmeldrum, north-east of Aberdeen. Buchan had never been much of a general; however, if Barbour is to be believed, Bruce was already viewed as an extraordinary military leader whose very presence was enough to cause doughty knights to turn tail.

And now he also showed his ruthless side, ordering his men to 'burn all Buchan from end to end, sparing none', an atrocity that was still remembered two generations later.[17] The earl, and other important families, fled across the border to England. It was the beginning of what would become a flood of Scottish refugees whom Edward II had to support.

King Robert almost certainly pursued his Scottish enemies over the winter of 1307–08 because he expected the English king to bring an army against him in the summer. He could not know that Edward would fail to return to Scotland until 1310, as English politics disintegrated in the face of the enormous debts left by his father and his own overwhelming reliance on inappropriate friends. When it became clear that there would be no campaign in 1308, Bruce was able to divide his army, sending part of it with Edward Bruce to Galloway to subdue that area and even take the war across the border. James Douglas, meanwhile, busied himself trying to recapture his family lands south-east of Glasgow.

The Scottish king stayed in the north, rampaging over mountains and through glens to terrorise his enemies, whether at Inverlochy (near current-day Fort William) in the far west, or at Urquhart and Inverness in the central highlands. Now he instituted another strand of his military strategy, this one quite revolutionary for the time. Each castle captured was to be destroyed, the walls pulled down and the well made unusable. Even James Douglas had to sleight his family home when he finally retrieved it, probably in 1309. Bruce had come to believe that these fortresses were of more use to his enemies than to himself.

King Robert found himself in a remarkably different position at the end of 1308 than he had at the beginning of the year. His armies seemed to be everywhere and, with each success, more people joined him, including men like the Earl of Ross, who 'must have reckoned that Bruce was unbeatable'.[18] The king was now able to give some attention to what, in normal circumstances, would have been the main business of government, and 1308 is the year that his chancellor, Bernard de Linton – the head of the royal chancery out of which documents were issued – first appears on record.

There is no doubt that, just as Bruce was lucky to escape capture in 1306 and 1307, he was fortunate in having Edward II as an adversary. The English king proved entirely incapable of managing the very difficult political situation he had inherited (though few would have been able to make a success of it). Bruce's Scottish enemies also proved to be no match for him either, lacking, as they were, any obvious leader or plan.

But Bruce was not just reacting to the weakness of his foes; rather, he was developing powerfully effective strategies – whether in battle, in raids or during and after sieges – to fight this multi-faceted war on his own terms. If he could not, as yet, capture walled towns like Perth or Berwick, then there was good reason to believe that it was only a matter of time before he found a way, especially if there were no English armies to trouble him. He could be brutal when clear messages needed to be sent, as the poor folk of Buchan found out to their cost. However, he could also be measured and generous, as when he not only confirmed the Earl of Ross in his own lands when he submitted, but granted him more into the bargain. This is all the more statesmanlike considering that Ross had been responsible for the capture of Bruce's wife and daughter and the brutal execution of his brother, Neil.

It was also now both possible and expedient for King Robert to hold his first parliament, which he duly summoned to St Andrews in March 1309. There his advisors began to tackle perhaps the thorniest problem of all: justifying to the international community how

Scotland could be ruled by an excommunicated murderer. It was a task these churchmen set to with relish and extraordinary skill.

Two documents were issued by those present at St Andrews, one from the magnates to the French king, Philip IV, and the other, known as the Declaration of the Clergy, from Scotland's churchmen. France still played host to the former Scottish king, John Balliol, who was living on his family lands in Picardy. Indeed, Philip had given money to John, whom he had called 'King of Scotland', as recently as 1308.

But now the French king wanted to go on crusade and he sought the help of the Scots, reminding them of the treaties between their two countries 'made long ago and confirmed', as well as 'the particular and special affection' in which he apparently held their new monarch. The Scots tactfully wrote back that there was still much to do before Scotland 'returns to its former free condition, the tempests of war having been quelled and secure peace having been granted', though they wished Philip well in his 'devout purpose'.

There is much that is disingenuous about this document, but there is also a degree of honesty – all the more telling, given that being honest was not the primary intention behind the exercise. It was admitted that 'the community of the realm of Scotland', which had been the key phrase when Scotland needed to speak with one voice since the death of King Alexander III, was now reduced to those 'recognising the fealty' of King Robert. There were, it was implicitly acknowledged, many others who could once have claimed to speak for that community but who now adhered to King Edward. Equally, there were those – the people of Buchan, Argyll and Galloway, for example, and individuals like the Earl of Strathearn – who had been brought into the Bruce camp only by the most brutal forms of persuasion.[19]

However, it is in the Declaration of the Clergy that the rewriting of history becomes entirely blatant. Its main purpose was to put forward a novel interpretation of the events of 1290–92, when Bruce's grandfather and John Balliol fought in Edward I's court to be judged King of Scotland. The Declaration alleged that 'the faithful people' had always believed Bruce the Competitor to be the 'true heir'. Thanks, however, to 'the various tricks and stratagems of rivals', he had been deprived of his rightful inheritance, as a result of which 'grave harm has since occurred to the kingdom of Scotland'. But, 'by the providence of the King most high', this wrong had been put right through his grandson, Robert I.

While making much of Bruce's credentials to be king by blood, considerable stress was also placed on his worthiness, and his possession of the 'cardinal virtues' that made him fit to govern. This was contrasted with Balliol, whose 'sins' had led to his deposition and Scotland being 'betrayed and reduced to slavery'. As a nod towards previous, equally fervent expressions of devotion to King John made by the Scots to the popes in particular, the Declaration asserted that these had been extorted 'by force and violence which it was then not possible to resist'.[20] Considering King Robert's recent military campaigns to compel large swathes of Scotland to accept his rule – something King John did not have to do – this was surely one of the more ironic statements in any piece of propaganda.

The unwary of Paris who were not old enough to remember the arguments about Scotland's recent history circulating a decade previously might well have concluded that justice had now been done to Bruce, whose grandfather's rights had been so peremptorily dismissed. The French were also being exhorted to understand that King Robert's ability to repair 'such a damaged and forsaken kingdom' by 'repelling injury with the sword' was just as important as his blood relationship to previous monarchs. In placing the needs of the kingdom alongside the rights of its king, the Scots were feeling their way towards a revolutionary new political ideal for medieval Europe. This would find its most effective and eloquent expression eleven years later in a letter sent by Scotland's nobility to the pope, now known as the Declaration of Arbroath. It would not be the first time nor the last that a great ideal has been forged in the bloody crucible of political necessity.

Both Declarations sought to justify an undeniably brutal and self-seeking change of regime. Yet the sentiments behind this special pleading had a particular resonance for the Scottish Church, which had spent over two centuries trying to maintain its independence from England. Having evolved out of the Celtic/Irish Church tradition before becoming assimilated into the ecclesiastical government presided over by Rome, Scotland's Church had no archbishops. The archbishops of England, York and Canterbury, were happy to extend their jurisdiction north, which led Scotland's bishops and other clergy to argue vociferously in Rome that they were in no way subject to the authority of the English Church. In 1192, the pope finally acknowledged the separate position of the Scottish Church, which he described as a 'special daughter no-one in between'.[21] Unfortunately he still refused to elevate a Scottish bishop to the position of archbishop, which would have solved the issue once and for all.

We should be careful not to equate the angst over the future of the apparently coherent notion of Scotland expressed so eloquently in the Declaration of the Clergy, and later in the Declaration of Arbroath, with a general and widespread belief in such a concept among the population at large. National identities were not particularly strong as yet throughout Western Europe. Regional identities remained extremely powerful, especially in a comparatively uncentralised kingdom like Scotland where monarchs rarely stuck their noses into the business of their earls and barons, whose primary task it was to get on with the nitty-gritty of governing their lands.

Indeed, what most people seem to have objected to when Edward I marched into Scotland and put in his own officials in 1296 was not his peremptory dismissal of the rights to self-governance of an independent kingdom (though that was certainly how churchmen like Robert Wishart of Glasgow saw it). Rather, it was the many and varied alterations he made to the status quo, whether that was removing Scotland's nobility from any role in royal government (and, on occasions, from their own lands) or demanding new services and a higher level of taxation from the landed classes in general. In other words, if the English king had allowed the Scots to get on with running themselves, as they had been doing for centuries, under his ultimate jurisdiction, there would probably have been far less resistance to the demise of Scotland's separate kingship.

However, by the end of the thirteenth century, conquest by kings like Edward I had come to mean assimilation – and assimilation meant resistance. As this seemingly interminable war became a way of life, and as the articulation of arguments in defence of Scotland's right to independence circulated among the elites, a more powerful sense of nationhood began to take hold.

5

The Unlikely Road to Bannockburn (1310–14)

... at the end of the 'suffraunce' [truce] at Midsummer purchased from Sir Robert de Bruys at his late coming, a truce of 15 days, and on his retreat, after they had returned to their houses, the next morning the warden and whole garrison of Berwick came and took their people in their beds, carrying them off dead and alive to Berwick, and held them to ransom, viz., on this foray within the Bounds of the earldom of Dunbar, both gentlemen and others, to the number of 30. Also 300 fat beasts, 4000 sheep, besides horses and dead stock.

Petition to Edward II,
Calendar of Documents relating to Scotland,
Vol. 3, 1884

Four years into King Robert's reign, despite his many successes, large swathes of Scotland remained in enemy hands. The city of Perth was still manned by a garrison paid for by Edward II, as were Stirling, Linlithgow, Edinburgh, Roxburgh and Berwick further south. In England, Edward's nobility made much of their king's inadequacies when it came to pursuing what was rightfully his, Scotland being part of that inheritance; but they were far from willing to give him the hard cash he needed to resume the war properly. In 1310, however, relations between Edward and his nobility reached such a nadir that the English king decided to remove himself from the maelstrom of discontent brewing in London by campaigning in Scotland. Edward's presence in and around Berwick for over a year gave new heart to Bruce's enemies and had the very welcome effect of ensuring that English garrisons were actually paid.

King Robert steadfastly refused to come out and fight, but did deem it worthwhile to send Edward II a letter on 1 October 1310, shortly after the English king came north. Its message was simple: listen to our pleas to make peace to save the shedding of Christian blood and we will give you anything you want that it is in our power to provide.[22] The tone is humble, even ingratiating – Edward is addressed at one point as 'your royal sublimity'. But King Robert still had little to lose, and everything to gain, in being obsequious to the only man who really mattered when it came to acknowledging his kingship and Scotland's independence. The only problem was that Edward believed as passionately in his right to rule Scotland as his father had done and the letter was ignored.

However, the English king could not skulk in Scotland forever. In September 1311, he returned south to face those, led by his cousin, Thomas, Earl of Lancaster, who opposed what they saw as his profligacy and mismanagement in general, and his devotion to the Gascon[23] Piers Gaveston, recently made Earl of Cornwall, in particular. Gaveston actually proved an effective commander while with King Edward in Scotland, taking charge at Perth in order to stop Bruce from crossing the River Forth en route to the north-east. But this made not even a dent in the disdain in which he was held by England's nobility.

Once the royal party had returned to London, English-held garrisons were again reduced to a hand-to-mouth existence. They were also largely unable to prevent Bruce and his men from coming south to target those communities and towns that still refused to acknowledge him as king. It was the beginning of a new policy, based on blackmail and intimidation, intended partly to swell King Robert's war chest and partly to demoralise the local population. He cared little whether those he targeted lived north or south of the border.

The south-east of Scotland had, by 1312, been under English control for sixteen years and was now the only real focus for resistance to King Robert within the northern kingdom. Unfortunately this put its inhabitants in an impossible position, neither wholly trusted nor protected no matter which side they chose. On the one hand, they faced the Scottish king's demands for money to leave them alone; on the other, the English king's officials constantly suspected that they were harbouring the enemy.

While most of England's nobility plotted to rid themselves, one way or another, of the hated Gaveston, King Edward seemed to be largely incapable of protecting his people in either kingdom. Indeed, he had occasion to admonish his own officials, albeit to little effect, for harassing those they were supposedly there to protect. Over the following years, Scottish raiders pushed further and further south through Northumberland and on even into Yorkshire, before returning back north, either directly through south-eastern Scotland or via Annandale after crossing west over the Pennines. Bruce generally preferred to make agreements that would enrich him and his cause, but where there was resistance or a need to make an example, the Scots would plunder.

Mounted on sturdy but fast ponies ideally suited to the high, rough ground of the border country, they were becoming the epitome of hardiness and discipline 'with the capacity to strike deep into the heart of enemy territory and to fight a battle on foot there if necessary'.[24] Even laden with booty and a slow-moving train of cattle, few dared to confront them. It was this kind of lightly armoured, highly mobile warfare that the English would eventually learn from and become masters of in their own right during their wars with France. But for now there was only the rarest prospect of an English army marching north, and even if it did, experience would suggest that it would sooner or later find it prudent to retreat without any form of tangible victory. Partly by his own guerrilla tactics but also by default, King Robert had gained the military upper hand.

His successes, too, were recognised further afield. The Scottish king was slowly transforming himself from a bandit pariah in the eyes of the international community into a ruler with whom it might be worth doing business. The treaty made between Scotland and Norway in October 1312 was both an acknowledgement of the long-standing relationship between the two countries (as well as the marriage between Alexander III of Scotland's daughter and King Eric II of Norway, Bruce's sister, Isobel, was Queen Dowager of the Scandinavian kingdom) and recognition that King Robert now possessed sufficient royal attributes to be formally recognised as a bona fide monarch.[25] And while King Philip stopped considerably short of a treaty, France was, as we have seen, in diplomatic correspondence with the Scottish king, much to the annoyance of Philip's son-in-law, Edward II of England. All that remained was to clear Scotland of the last few English garrisons and the war was surely effectively, if not formally, over.

However, removing English garrisons was certainly not easy. As Earl of Carrick, Bruce had supplied Edward I with 'engines' to help with the siege of Stirling Castle in 1304.[26] Since at least 1308, however, ladders had become the low-tech mainstay of his own conquest of Scotland. These proved remarkably effective, not least because they could be moved around easily and quietly, maintaining the element of surprise. Even mighty Berwick – remodelled and largely re-walled by Edward I – might well have succumbed to them in December 1312 if a dog had not barked, just as geese had once saved Rome.

The besiegers promptly ran off, leaving their ladders behind, thus allowing the English a good look at these devices, which they had to admit were 'of wonderful construction'. In essence they were little more than two long pieces of rope with a knot at each end separated by wooden boards capable of holding a man. At the top of each rope were two iron hooks, one limb pointing upwards to attach to the wall. The other end pointed down and was hollow at the bottom to allow Bruce's men to push a spear into them to lift the hooks over the wall. The final refinement was the addition, at intervals, of wooden cushioning devices to ensure that the ladders did not lie flat against the battlements.[27]

Such a tactic – known as *escalade* – was an accepted, if basic, strategy in medieval siege warfare but was usually only employed if the besiegers were sufficiently numerous to risk the inevitable casualties in an attempt to reach and open the main gate from the inside. As we will see, under

King Robert the humble ladder became a key weapon in its own right and there is no doubt that those it was used against had reason to view the tactic with both wonder and fear. The Scots under Bruce were beginning to prove consistently that limited resources were no barrier to success if combined with imagination, discipline and bravery. Edward II, by contrast – distraught and vengeful after the judicial murder of Piers Gaveston in June 1312 by several of England's earls – was accused of throwing Scotland away through neglect.

After the failure at Berwick, Bruce turned his attention on Perth. The town lies on the banks of the stately River Tay just before it turns sharply east towards the North Sea. An ancient settlement less than 3 miles south of the inauguration site at Scone, it jealously guarded its trading privileges from the town of Dundee at the mouth of the Tay Estuary. Dundee had surrendered to King Robert at Easter 1312, leaving Perth, surrounded by a stone wall, as the last major impediment to Bruce's control of Scotland north of the River Forth.

The garrison commander was Sir William Oliphant who, nine years previously, had held out against Edward I at Stirling in the name of King John. He proved equally resistant to Bruce's attempts to dislodge him and the Scottish king was forced to recognise that the walls were unlikely to fall by 'open attack, force or assault'. So he decided to use guile.

Despite the fact that it was deepest January 1313, Bruce got his men to test the waters of the ditch beneath the walls before finding a point where they could wade across up to their shoulders. They then pretended to raise the siege, to howls of derision from those inside, before returning on foot several days later, armed with wooden ladders. King Robert, determined to lead by example, waded into the icy waters first. This earned the astonished admiration of a Frenchman in his force, who declared that no French lord, 'willing only to eat, drink and dance', would have risked his life 'to win a wretched hamlet'. The king's bravado duly encouraged his men, who plunged in with the ladders and promptly scaled the wall. After the destruction of the gates, the rest of Bruce's men swarmed in and took what they liked from the terrified citizens.[28]

Contemporary sources are uncertain about King Robert's treatment of the people of Perth. One chronicler says that the 'better class' of Scots in the town were killed, while the English there were allowed to go free. Another claims that the 'disloyal people' of both nations were slaughtered, but those who sought clemency were granted it. A third suggests that death and destruction were unleashed because the townspeople refused terms, while Barbour says that 'few were slain' for the very good reason that their relatives lived in the surrounding countryside and would be likely to retaliate.[29]

There is no doubt that Bruce would not shy away from dealing out death and destruction when necessary; but he had learned to think very carefully about the possible consequences. If he did allow his men to kill, then the discipline that he had nurtured in them since his return to mainland Scotland in 1307 ensured that it did not become gratuitous. By now many of them were, in effect, mercenaries who expected to be well rewarded for their efforts. In return, they did as they were told.

With Perth successfully captured, King Robert could now turn his attention to the south. The pele (a structure surrounded by a wooden palisade) of Linlithgow reputedly fell to him in September 1313 when 'stalwart' William Bunnock, a local man, brought his hay cart full of armed men to a halt beneath the main gate, whereupon they jumped out and slaughtered the surprised garrison.[30] Putting pressure on the remaining English strongholds was now an important part of what the king presumably hoped would be the endgame for the war in Scotland. This phase was effectively launched in October 1313 with an ultimatum that all those holding lands in his kingdom must swear homage and fealty to him within the year or lose them.

This, together with recent appeals for help from landowners in south-east Scotland, had a galvanising effect on the English king, who finally realised that he had to bring an army north or risk the end of resistance to Bruce within Scotland itself. On 23 December, writs of summons were issued, ordering his troops to assemble at Berwick on 10 June 1314.

Meanwhile, it was the Scottish king's generals who vied with one another to employ the most innovative strategies to reduce castles before Edward's army arrived. On the night of the Feast of Shrove Tuesday (19/20 February),

25-year-old James Douglas and his men donned black surcoats over their armour and crawled up to the walls of the great castle of Roxburgh, only a few miles from the border, to avoid detection. They then quickly scaled their ladders and surprised the garrison, who were enjoying the feast day.

Sir Thomas Randolph, Bruce's nephew and the Earl of Moray, was already besieging Edinburgh Castle, atop its rocky eyrie, but was stung into a new strategy by Douglas' success at Roxburgh. Barbour describes Randolph as 'wise, worthy and brave, and of such supreme courage that much might be said of him'. He was also more handsome than Douglas, being 'of moderate stature and well-formed in proportion, with a broad face, pleasant and fair, courteous and debonair in all respects and of assured demeanour'. Using local knowledge of a secret pathway up the castle rock and effecting a decoy attack on the south gate, Randolph and his men, like Douglas, used the cover of darkness to scale the walls of Edinburgh Castle with ladders and overpower the garrison before destroying the fortifications on 14 March.[31]

Now the only royal castles left in enemy hands were Stirling and Berwick. King Robert decided to tackle Stirling next. Its castle, like Edinburgh's, sits on a rocky outcrop rising above the floodplain of the River Forth as it loops its way to its tidal limit. Guarding the main north–south route across the Forth and overlooked by hills to the north and dramatic mountains to the west, Stirling is 'like a huge brooch, clasps Highlands and Lowlands together'.[32]

6

The Exception that Proved the Rule (1314)

You could have lived in serfdom.
But, because you yearned to have freedom,
You are gathered here with me.

Bruce's speech before Bannockburn,
in John Barbour, *The Bruce*, 2007

In mid-April 1314, Edward Bruce, who had taken over command of the siege from his brother, came to an agreement with the commander of Stirling Castle, Sir Philip Moubray (surely with the king's approval[33]). The Scots were unwilling to waste time sitting around while an English army was preparing to march north – for a start, each noble commander needed to attend to the muster of the men of their own areas. Bruce himself, who had left the siege probably in order to train his men in a nearby wood, was surely intent on bringing Edward II to a place of his own choosing. In any event, it was agreed that the castle would be handed over to King Robert if not relieved by midsummer.

Moubray was then allowed to go and inform King Edward, by now in Northumberland on his way north, of this agreement. Stirling, then, would be the English army's objective, though it would need to move swiftly to meet the deadline. Moubray duly pointed out to his royal master the difficult terrain for cavalry in the castle's vicinity and warned that Bruce was known to be gathering his own men nearby. Edward understood and sent out orders that foot soldiers should be sent north in large numbers.

It is difficult, when discussing such an iconic battle as Bannockburn, not to be influenced by hindsight. This has less to do with the actual outcome, though that was certainly astonishing, and more to do with the fact that the English certainly did not expect that they would ever come to blows. Although he had not taken on an English army since 1307, King Robert had good reasons to fight this time. Having come so close to expelling his enemies entirely from Scotland and with his own ultimatum waiting to expire, retreating would, on this occasion, seriously weaken his position and prolong the need to reconquer his kingdom. This did not mean that the Scottish king had entirely made up his mind; only that he did consider battle to be a possibility for once and found it prudent to prepare for it.

Reputedly taking his men into the large expanse of woodland between the River Carron and the Tor Burn, south of Stirling, King Robert set to work on this, his ultimate challenge. At Falkirk in 1298, Wallace had roped in his schiltroms – hedgehog-like formations of spearmen – facing downhill in a fundamentally defensive position. His aim had been to repel a heavy cavalry charge, but the schiltroms ended up defenceless when Edward I unleashed both archers *and* horse. Bruce now drilled his men to take the offensive, to march together with spears bristling – an obviously difficult and dangerous manoeuvre. Archers might still prove difficult to deal with, but at least the Scots would not be sitting ducks.

As Edward II and his army were leaving Edinburgh on 22 June, King Robert moved back towards Stirling from the Torwood to camp in the New Park – a royal hunting reserve[34] – in order to block the English approach to the castle. The Scottish king ordered his men to dig ditches or pits on either side of the road, just as they had done at Loudoun Hill, to keep the English cavalry from spreading out. Then they waited.

Edward arrived in the nick of time on 23 June, but his foot soldiers were much the worse for their quick march north. His inability to manage either men or strategy was already proving divisive: the Earl of Hereford, whose family traditionally commanded the vanguard, strenuously protested the king's decision to award the role to the Earl of Gloucester.

Under the terms of the agreement, the castle was relieved, but Edward was scarcely going to leave the matter there, knowing, thanks to Moubray, that the Scots were marshalling for retreat in the forest ahead. But, despite his earlier acknowledgement of the need to use infantry against Bruce's spearmen, the English king had no coherent strategy to throw at the enemy other than a basic cavalry charge.

Perhaps the most famous – and dramatic – moment of the entire affair was the first. As the English began to ride pell-mell towards the Scots, a knight, usually identified as Sir Henry de Bohun, recognised the Scottish king, busy organising his men, by the crown upon his helmet. Spotting a glorious opportunity, the 'noble' knight charged straight towards Bruce, who in turn did not hesitate to 'set his horse towards him'. De Bohun, on his great warhorse, 'missed the noble king' mounted on a palfrey. Bruce then rose in his stirrups and dealt him such a mighty blow with his axe 'that he cleaved the head to his brains'. A mighty cheer erupted from the Scots, though Bruce's generals supposedly chided him for endangering his life, to which the future of his dynasty clung so fragilely. But it was hardly the first time he had led from the front.

The rest of the English horse failed to break through Scottish lines. Neither did a cavalry force under the veteran Sir Robert Clifford and Sir Henry Beaumont, who had inherited a claim to the earldom of Buchan through his wife, Alice, niece of Earl John Comyn. They tried to ride between Bruce and the castle – perhaps in order to cut off his escape route – before being repulsed by Sir Thomas Randolph's men. The schiltroms yet again held firm, astonishing and bemusing the flower of English chivalry. By late afternoon, King Edward gave the order to find shelter and water down on the floodplain of the Forth, away from the possibility of a Scottish night attack.

In the Scottish camp, morale was high, but King Robert was still not convinced that the odds were sufficiently in his favour; the possibility of losing this battle now no doubt weighed upon Bruce's mind as a more dangerous option than withdrawing. It was a Scottish defector from Edward's army, Sir Alexander Seton, bearing tales of English disarray and demoralisation, who persuaded the Scottish king that it was worth fighting. In the end, Bruce asked his men to decide, giving an impassioned speech on the subject of liberty – 'You could have lived in serfdom. But, because you yearned to have freedom, you are gathered here with me' – as well as promising more pragmatically that, should they die, their heirs would inherit without paying the Crown its customary dues.[35]

King Edward and his nobles, many of whom had considerable experience in Scotland, remained confident, not least that battle was still unlikely. The next morning, however, Bruce's men could be seen approaching in three brigades. The Scottish king had taken advantage of these unusually chivalrous conditions to knight young Turks like James Douglas and Walter Stewart, son of the James Stewart who had been party to Bruce's first patriotic foray back in 1297. After Bruce had given another stirring speech invoking the saints, and the Scots had knelt ostentatiously in prayer, Edward Bruce's schiltrom suddenly advanced, catching the astonished English off guard.

The Earl of Gloucester immediately rushed off to lead the English vanguard to meet them. Bruce had been most explicit, when the decision to fight was taken, that none should take either plunder or prisoners before the battle was clearly won. The former had precedents in warfare, but the latter seems to have been another of the Scottish king's innovations. He needed his men to maintain their discipline and focus so that 'you will surely have victory'.[36] And so, obeying their king's command, the Scots pressed on. Gloucester was killed in the thick of the fighting, along with Sir Robert Clifford, who had campaigned in Scotland for nearly twenty years, Sir John Comyn, son of the man Bruce killed, and many others. The English were hemmed in by the Pelstream to their right and the Bannockburn to their left, unable to spread out and dominate the field.

Many fought bravely on the English side that day, but without any clear plan or chain of command they were no match for the disciplined, well-organised Scots. Even the Scottish cavalry proved useful, keeping the English archers at bay. King Edward was no coward, having to be forced off the field by his nobles, but he was no general either. Sir Philip Moubray refused to let him into Stirling Castle, perhaps knowing that he could no longer keep the English king safe from Bruce. But he may also have felt shame and embarrassment – a sense that Edward no longer deserved his protection.

With their king gone and a new army of 'sma folk'[37] supposedly careering into view, the English army fell apart. Each man now found himself in his own desperate struggle to avoid death (if a foot soldier) or capture for ransom (if a nobleman). As Bruce had promised his men, 'at your pleasure, you may take all the riches that are there' once victory was assured.[38] So thorough was this clean-up operation that archaeologists have only recently found anything at all that Bruce's men might have missed. Even so, the general lack of material evidence, combined with the ambiguity of the primary sources, has led to considerable disagreement as to the precise location of the battle – a dispute that, alas, is unlikely to be resolved.

But what surely matters most is the fact that King Robert had won a battle which, according to a fundamental principle of medieval society, should not have been possible. For his sins alone, it was difficult to fathom how God could have granted him victory. Nor did the normal rules of war anticipate such a rout of mounted knights, led by King Edward himself, by lowly spearmen. In England the soul-searching that inevitably followed upon such an unequivocal and humiliating defeat focused on the arrogance of Edward and his generals in presuming far too much on their supposed natural superiority and their lack of humility in not seeking God's blessing – most easily achieved by stopping at various shrines en route – as Edward I used to do.[39]

Seven hundred years later, it is hard not to agree. It should certainly have been possible to realise – and indeed Edward seems to have known this – that a reliance on cavalry was no longer a guarantee of victory against well-disciplined foot soldiers, especially on what was effectively ground of their own choosing. Intelligent leaders of infantry in medieval Europe were developing techniques to beat horsemen: using and manipulating terrain to make it less amenable to large-scale cavalry charges, and providing appropriate training and organisation to give their men the courage and confidence to hold fast when confronted with a ground-shaking assault from mounted knights. And whether his enemies liked it or not, it was obvious that Bruce was one of the most intelligent, innovative and adept generals of the age, whose exploits were helping to forge a new kind of warfare. Although cavalry would remain integral to successful military strategy right up into the twentieth century, from now on it was only 'as part of a combined arms team'.[40]

There was another, rather more abstract development that Bruce was clearly taking advantage of too. In his speech before the battle seeking to persuade his lords to fight, they replied with the promise that 'nor shall any effort be refused till we have made our country free!'[41] While this may be a sentiment that chimes with modern instincts, it was a radical notion for the Middle Ages, when land was held across borders as a matter of course and the pope warned of the dangers of nationalism as a challenge to the international community of the Christian faithful.

Robert the Bruce did not invent Scottish nationalism – if it had not already existed, however loosely defined, then the war between Scotland and England would surely never have broken out. And, despite the communitarian rhetoric, it is not surprising that the violence and disruption caused by the conflict may have engendered sharper regional loyalties in some parts of Scotland, in contrast to the increasing assimilation evident before the outbreak of war.

Nevertheless, Bruce seems to have been able to articulate quite brilliantly and simply – and this Bannockburn speech, though written down later, appears to have been his own, authentic words – a notion of collective belief in the paramount right of a nation to remain independent of any external power. Despite his own dubious track record leading up to his seizure of the throne, the Scottish king and his advisors were developing a rhetoric which made it clear that he and his followers occupied the moral high ground against those who would 'destroy us all'.[42]

In the words themselves, and in the camaraderie evident in the offer to his nobles that they should choose whether or not to fight, we glimpse a man of great charisma. Here was someone who understood how to sway others with his oratory, someone who could speak to their hearts. And however much of a public relations exercise this certainly was, it is quite possible that by now Bruce believed every word of it himself.

There is no doubt that victory at Bannockburn boosted his status, news of it resounding around Europe. The French chronicler Jean le Bel, who described Bruce as *'le proeu roy d'Escoce de ce siecle'* ('the most valiant Scottish king of this century'), commented that he 'discomfited this king [Edward II] and all the barons of England ... in pitched battle'. He even admitted that this was not really the subject matter of his book, but clearly found mentioning it irresistible.[43] However, the main impact of the battle was felt in Scotland itself. King Robert could and did enforce his ultimatum, and many now knew for certain that King Edward could do nothing to help them. This included Sir Ingram d'Umfraville, who, as a friend of the Comyns, had replaced Bruce as Guardian in 1300. Such men had little choice, therefore, but to accept Bruce as their king.

Of perhaps the greatest immediate significance was the capture of many high-ranking English noblemen. The

Earl of Hereford alone prompted a prisoner exchange that included the ancient Bishop Wishart of Glasgow, the only slightly less venerable Bishop Lamberton of St Andrews and all of Robert's womenfolk.

Eighteen-year-old Marjory, the king's only child, was heir apparent. But upon her return from imprisonment in April 1315, parliament met and agreed, apparently with her consent, that Edward Bruce, Earl of Carrick, would become king if Robert died without a male heir. This had surely been the understanding, however informally, already reached by the Bruce brothers. Edward was deemed the right choice to lead the kingdom in these difficult times 'as a vigorous man and tested on many occasions in acts of war for the defence of the right and liberty of the kingdom of Scotland'.[44] It is a sad testament to the impact of years of conflict that Scotland, which had been on the brink of accepting a female monarch only twenty-five years earlier, could no longer contemplate one.

Marjory still had a vital role to play, however. She was immediately married to Walter Stewart and in 1316 gave birth to King Robert's grandson, named in his honour, at the cost of her own life. Edward Bruce remained his brother's heir, though his chances of taking the throne diminished with the birth of a grandson to the king, who himself also soon hoped to have a son of his own.

For many, perhaps most, Scots it must have seemed that, to all intents and purposes, Bannockburn marked the end of the war. Only Berwick remained in English hands and, after November 1314, most Scottish landholders who could possibly be reconciled to King Robert were. So far as Bruce himself was concerned, however, the war was not over until Edward II sealed a document acknowledging both Scotland's independence and his own rightful kingship. Such a peace treaty Bannockburn had manifestly failed to deliver. It was time to think even bigger.

7

Piling on the Pressure (1315–26)

At the same time the Scots entered by way of Carlisle, and rode far into England, when the common people of the towns and the people of Holy Church assembled at Myton, and were there defeated, as a folk unaccustomed to war and in disorderly array before fierce troops.

The Scalacronica of Sir Thomas Gray, 1907

King Robert had won a resounding victory and was now master of all Scotland (bar Berwick) and, in effect, swathes of northern England. Even so, Edward II, safe in the far south, had no inclination to make peace. Indeed, it would have been considered a serious abrogation of his responsibilities as king to have done so. This surely best explains why, shortly after he was named his brother's heir in 1315, Edward Bruce left Scotland with an army bound for Ireland where, a year later, he was proclaimed High King by the native Irish nobility.

Historians have long argued over the precise purpose of this remarkable venture, largely because of the assertion of John of Fordun (writing in the 1360s and repeated by Barbour) that 'Edward was a very mettlesome and high-spirited man and would not dwell together with his brother in peace, unless he had half the kingdom for himself; and for this reason this war was stirred up in Ireland'.[45] Were it the case that the Scottish king's younger brother was motivated solely by a burning desire for a crown of his own, then it is remarkable that both Bruce himself and Sir Thomas Randolph also crossed the Irish Sea to help him win it, leaving Scotland potentially exposed.

That Edward Bruce was rash and impetuous may well have been true, but this Irish expedition has King Robert's mail glove prints all over it. In targeting Ireland – a possession of the English kings since 1155 – the Bruce brothers were threatening King Edward on a second front. They were also dangling the possibility of what is usually described as a pan-Celtic alliance, which might spread to include Wales, raising the prospect of an England surrounded by enemies.

There is no doubt that the English king took this threat very seriously. A major crisis of resources, resulting from an outbreak of famine and cattle disease across Europe from 1315 onwards, meant that he effectively had to choose between supporting his men in Berwick, the last remaining stronghold in Scotland, or Ireland. Early in 1316, it was Ireland that was deemed more important, despite the 'great distress' in the Scottish town, though an unsuccessful attempt by an English army to relieve Berwick was made in 1317.[46]

These terrible conditions also affected Edward Bruce's invasion, soon transforming any kindred spirit felt by the native Irish towards the Scots into bitter animosity as food began to run out. Although Edward Bruce did win battles and some territory, largely with the help of Thomas Randolph, he could not take Dublin. In October 1318, he was slain in a battle at Faughart, just north of Dundalk, and the four quarters of his body were sent to various parts of Ireland. He was mourned by few in his supposed kingdom. His reputation is difficult to evaluate because of the horrific conditions of those years and a tendency by later chroniclers to blame anything that might rebound to discredit King Robert on him, often quite unjustifiably.[47]

After Bannockburn it has been rightly stated that King Robert enjoyed 'an unparalleled Scottish military hegemony in Britain'.[48] Also, although the Scots failed to take Carlisle despite a great effort in 1315, much of the north of England was effectively lost to Edward II. Nevertheless, the failure of the Irish venture – and the great distress that was inextricably linked with this period – brought misery to Scotland too and new problems for King Robert. In 1318 the Scottish parliament was forced to act to stop those tempted to be 'a conspirator or an inventor of tales or rumours by which a source of discord shall be able to arise between the lord king and his people'.

This was the first parliament where Bruce was either willing or able to make a concerted effort to get to grips, through legislation, with a plethora of domestic business – something that, under normal circumstances, a ruler would have been wise to deal with rather sooner. Much of it was a reiteration of previous statute, but some of it was an attempt to deal with the lawlessness and violence that was now as much a part of life in Scotland as it was in northern England.[49]

To what extent was King Robert to blame? That is a difficult question to answer. As Winston Churchill found out to his cost after the Second World War, even the greatest military leaders can prove unequal to the challenges of peace. Certainly it is not difficult to imagine that the very reasons why Bruce was on top militarily – his single-mindedness, his unerring focus on the next move, his reliance on the loyalty and prowess of his lieutenants and their men – were also likely to cause problems for his subjects more generally once they could turn away from the immediate needs of the war. Above all it was difficult to get justice when the king's attention was so often focused elsewhere, and when many of those behaving badly were likely to be the very men whom Bruce had armed, trained and taught to attack, rob and kill even other Scots, if necessary.

It was also becoming abundantly clear that the fact that King Robert and his generals could run rings around King Edward in the field – Berwick was captured by the Scots in 1318 and an English 'relief' army was easily repulsed the following year – was becoming less and less relevant as warfare in Scotland dwindled away. Moreover, there was one particular ghost that Bruce could never lay to rest, no matter how many battles he won.

King John's son, Edward Balliol, had not been allowed to accompany his father into exile. Instead he remained in England in 'leisurely captivity' and eventually became effectively an English lord, albeit of impoverished means.[50] At some point after Bannockburn, he returned to his ancestral lands in Picardy, his father having died in November 1314. Nevertheless, Edward II had long realised his potential usefulness in his war with King Robert and Balliol, by now in his early thirties, returned to England to take part in the abortive attempt to recover Berwick in 1319.

Despite the triumphant and deterministic rhetoric of Scottish chronicles, King Robert remained a murderer and a usurper in the minds of many Scots, however much God had rewarded him at Bannockburn. Edward Balliol, on the other hand, had an unimpeachable claim to the Scottish throne for some, though his closeness to and dependence on the English king made him unpalatable to others.

The presence of an alternative claimant to the throne of Scotland lurking south of the border might have remained of purely academic interest had it not been for the death of Edward Bruce and the repercussions of the decision to take Berwick in 1318. Pope John XXII was planning a crusade and, to that end, had ordered the Kings of England and Scotland to desist from fighting each other. Needless to say, Bruce had no intention of halting attempts to reduce the last Scottish stronghold in English hands, despite knowing that he risked the excommunication of his entire kingdom.

Anticipating papal censure, King Robert assembled his great men and proposed that, as in 1309, a document should be drawn up detailing the reasons why Scotland needed to fight England and highlighting Bruce's role in leading the Scots in their quest for freedom. Over the coming months, the seals of fifty-one nobles were attached to the document, which was duly sent to the pope. A subsequent presumption that its contents were drafted by the Scottish chancellor, Bernard of Kilwinning, means that it has come to be known as the Declaration of Arbroath, after the abbey of which he was abbot.

The Declaration is an exquisitely crafted expression of the right of a nation to its freedom. It is also a deliberate falsification of Scotland's history, both recent and more remote, that nevertheless resulted in the articulation of a revolutionary idea for the Middle Ages. The Declaration states categorically that should King Robert 'give up what he has begun, seeking to make us or our kingdom subject to the King of England or the English, we should exert ourselves at once to drive him out as our enemy and a subverter of his own right and ours, and make some other man who was well able to defend us our King'.[51]

We should not forget – any more than those who sealed it would have done – that Bruce was the ultimate architect of this document and that he had neither the desire nor the opportunity to take such an inconceivable course of action. This was not an argument being put forward for its own sake, but one to overcome a major objection to Robert I's kingship: his extremely dubious claim to the throne by blood. Yet we should not dismiss the possibility that those who drafted it, along with many of the men in whose name the Declaration was written – those who had shared the desperate first years of Bruce's reign and ridden long and hard with him since – really did believe that Scotland's right to be independent was more important than the right of any individual to be king, if he would not or could not fulfil that difficult task. It was fitness for the job rather than the closest relationship by blood to the previous incumbent that had, after all, dictated who should become king in the early centuries of that institution in Europe.

Unfortunately for King Robert, there were others who did not share this view. As we have seen, as early as 1318, when the future of the Bruce dynasty suddenly rested on the tiny shoulders of 2-year-old Robert Stewart, there were 'conspirators' or 'inventors of tales or rumours' still willing to look elsewhere for a 'true' King of Scots. Even as the Declaration was being carried to the pope, a number of Scottish nobles who had sealed it may have been meeting with Edward Balliol in France. It was certainly in France that Patrick, Earl of Dunbar and one of the Declaration's bearers, heard rumours of a plot to assassinate King Robert and replace him.[52] Dunbar relayed the news back to Scotland, where action against the suspected conspirators was swift and uncompromising. Sir Ingram d'Umfraville, the former Guardian, was supposedly so disgusted by the execution of Sir David Brechin in particular (who had not been party to the conspiracy but knew of it and said nothing) that he sold his lands in Scotland and went to live on his French estates, informing the king that 'My heart does not allow me to be any longer with you, living in this country.'[53] He may, however, have been pre-empting his own trial and execution.

The truth is that, like any usurper no matter how successful and charismatic, Robert the Bruce would never be wholly acceptable to a section of Scotland's political community. He was fortunate indeed, in 1320, that King Edward was unable to co-ordinate with those involved in this plot, for that would have been extremely serious. Sealing the Declaration may well have only served to remind some that Bruce did not, by the strict laws of succession, have the best claim to be king. And yet there were others, like Patrick of Dunbar – finally reconciled to King Robert following Bannockburn despite a consistent family history of loyalty to the English kings – who thought enough of him to stay loyal when it really mattered.

Meanwhile, Edward II's relationship with his cousin, Thomas of Lancaster – who had taken charge of England's government on and off since Bannockburn – was reaching crisis point. War finally broke out between them in 1321. Sir Andrew Harclay, who was usually responsible for the defence of Carlisle against the Scots, defeated Lancaster and Hereford at Boroughbridge in North Yorkshire in March 1322. He did so by placing his unmounted knights and pikemen at one end of the bridge across the River Ure and arranging more pikemen 'in schiltrom, after the Scottish fashion' to guard the ford in order 'to oppose the cavalry wherein the enemy put his trust'.[54] Harclay, who had been at Bannockburn and also had considerable experience against Bruce's raiding parties, was learning important lessons from fighting the Scots.

Lancaster and his allies having been dealt with, Edward II was determined to do as he pleased. Harclay – now Earl of Carlisle – realised that he served a king incapable of ruling consistently or effectively and turned to King Robert in 1323, determined to make a peace that would save the north of England from the endemic warfare that plagued it. Unsurprisingly, King Edward viewed this as lese-majesty, and had the precocious earl executed;

however, he made his own peace with the Scottish king only two months later.

This was not a final treaty, but it at least promised to put an end to cross-border warfare for the considerable period of thirteen years. Most importantly, the agreement was binding on both governments if either king died. Since Bruce was older, and rumoured to be ailing, this was a considerable relief, as Robert Stewart would be a man of 20 by the time the treaty expired. A final peace was as far away as ever, however, for the simple reason that King Edward could not bring himself to sign away English claims to suzerainty over Scotland.

Nevertheless, these were surely much better years for King Robert, who was now in his fifties. With his borders secure at last, he could turn to domestic matters. From 1318, parliaments were held every year (apart from 1322). Bruce seems not to have been particularly interested in legislation, but he did recognise the need to be proactive in land disputes, which were very close to the hearts and livelihoods of his subjects (and a considerable headache now that so many estates had been forfeited and so much land redistributed). The Scottish king had long been aware of the need to reward his supporters with lands taken from those who opposed him, at the risk of permanently alienating the latter. This thorny issue would come back to plague Anglo-Scottish relations for generations to come.

In November 1324, at Berwick, the king presided over a series of ceremonies that must have pleased him greatly. Three of his closest friends and lieutenants – Sir Robert

Keith, who had commanded the cavalry at Bannockburn, Sir James Douglas and Bruce's nephew, Thomas Randolph, Earl of Moray – all resigned their lands to him and were regranted them. For Douglas and Moray, this regrant effectively raised their lands to the status of a regality, where royal officials could not interfere except in restricted circumstances. Moreover, 'the Good' Sir James received his lands back with the gift of an emerald – a touching and permanent reminder of his king's gratitude and goodwill.[55]

Bruce had plenty of reasons to be generous; eight months earlier, on 5 March 1324, Queen Elizabeth had given birth to twin boys, one of whom survived. He was named David, no doubt after their illustrious royal ancestor, David I. And two months before that, the pope had acknowledged Bruce as King of Scotland – a remarkable achievement considering John XXII's public antipathy to him only a few years previously. Although King Robert did have significant unfinished business with England, he might well have considered that he had achieved almost everything that was humanly possible. Peace was guaranteed until 1336, by which time his dynasty, reliant not on one but two little boys, would be much more firmly established.

Two years later, once David had proved sufficiently robust, the succession was formally settled on him and, in the event that he had no heirs, Robert Stewart. It was reiterated from 1316 that if King Robert died while either was still too young to rule, Thomas Randolph, Earl of

Moray, would act as Guardian. At the same time, and despite the tribute coming in from England, the Scottish Crown faced a financial crisis because so much of the land that traditionally funded its rental income had been given away. Bruce was driven to negotiate for money with his political community in order to stop demands for various 'prises' – one-off levies of foodstuffs that were deeply unpopular.

To some extent this was a reflection of Bruce's pragmatism; any new dynasty, but especially one that came to power in such controversial circumstances, needs to bind to it a loyal cohort capable of dealing with areas unreconciled to the new regime through a proper system of reward. In this case, the results were transformative: 'his landed patronage represented a restructuring of the nobility, reforming the political class in his own image and interest.'[56] However, there was a fine line between being generous and jeopardising his own position. The earls, barons and burgesses agreed to give him a tenth of their incomes every year for the rest of the king's life, but it was made very clear that this was a response to special circumstances; he and his successors were not to presume that they were entitled to levy it as of right.[57]

Meanwhile in England, Edward II's newest favourites, the Despensers, threatened to destabilise the Plantagenet kingdom far more effectively than Piers Gaveston had ever done. And they vastly overplayed their hand when they alienated Queen Isabella, who was sister to the French king, Charles IV. Even more foolishly, Edward allowed

Isabella to go to France in March 1325 to negotiate with her brother over the English king's duchy of Gascony, taking their son, 12-year-old Prince Edward, with her. Once there, she made contact with those exiled English nobles opposed to the Despensers and promised that her son would marry Philippa of Hainault in return for mercenaries from the girl's father, Count William.

Isabella's tiny army landed in England in September 1326. Her husband immediately tried to summon a force against her, but quickly found out how hated his regime now was. Within a month, London was not safe either for the king or the Despensers, while support for the queen gathered pace. Finally, on 16 November 1326, King Edward was captured in Wales, perhaps en route for Ireland. Both Despensers were brutally executed and Edward was imprisoned in Kenilworth Castle while the new government under Isabella and her lover, Roger Mortimer, Lord of Wigmore, decided what to do with him. On 20 January, having heard the charges against him – which included the loss of Scotland – Edward II tearfully abdicated in favour of his son. Although he managed to escape briefly from Kenilworth during the summer, he died in Berkeley Castle, Gloucestershire, on 21 September 1327, most likely murdered to prevent another attempt at his restoration. It was even believed – irony of ironies – that Robert the Bruce, who was known to be ailing, was plotting to save his enemy, in return for Scotland's independence.[58]

8

The Search for Peace (1326–28)

I will, that as soon as I am dead, you take my heart from my body, and have it well embalmed; you will also take as much money from my treasury as will appear to you sufficient to perform your journey, as well as for all those you may choose to take with you in your train; You will then deposit your charge at the Holy Sepulchre of our Lord, where he was buried, since my body cannot go there. You will not be sparing of expense – and provide yourself with such company and such things as may be suitable for your rank – and wherever you pass, you will let it be known, that you bear the heart of king Robert of Scotland, which you are carrying beyond the seas at his command, since his body cannot go thither.

The Chronicles of Sir Jean Froissart,
fourteenth century

It is possible, in the last desperate days of Edward II's life, that King Robert was also offered the earldom of Ulster in return for help in restoring him to his throne. Queen Elizabeth's father, Richard, Earl of Ulster, died in July 1326 and, despite the English king's abdication a few weeks earlier, the Justiciar of Ireland sent a deputation to the Scottish king as early as February 1327, presumably sounding out the possibility of support. King Robert certainly crossed the Irish Sea between April and July, and did so by strength of character alone. Around the same time, it was said that Bruce was 'so feeble and so weak that he will not last much longer from this time, with the help of God, because he cannot move anything except his tongue'. Although the Scottish king was clearly very ill by now, he once more confounded his enemies. He returned home in August, having made very clear his interest in Ulster, but having failed to win over the Anglo-Irish to an invasion of England against the new regime.[59]

Meanwhile, and despite the 1323 truce, Randolph and Douglas tried the more direct approach, bringing their men flooding across the border from east and west. It was noted by one English chronicler that 'My lord Robert de Brus, who had become leprous, did not invade England on this occasion'.[60] It did not greatly matter. The regency government prepared to meet the Scottish army, bringing a force that included the young King Edward III himself to Durham in mid-July. After a game of cat and mouse, the Scots allowed themselves to be found at Stanhope, less than 30 miles south-west of Newcastle.

Douglas taunted the English, refusing to engage with them on the flat ground, then moved to a better position. During the night of 3–4 August, the infamous Scottish general attacked the English army, crying, 'Douglas, Douglas, you will all die, English lords!' The Scots succeeded in killing several hundred men, the Good Sir James even cutting the guy ropes of King Edward III's tent, prompting the 14-year-old to burst into tears of frustration and humiliation. No wonder English mothers at the time tried to induce their children to sleep by threatening that the Black Douglas would get them. Despite keeping a close watch, the English were powerless to prevent the Scots from slipping away back across the border. It was a deeply embarrassing incident that did nothing to endear Roger Mortimer, who was already known to be rewarding himself with lands and offices, to the people he now effectively ruled.[61]

King Robert and his generals now intervened directly in English affairs, putting pressure on the new government by threatening to take some of the border castles. By now the Scottish king was taking tribute as far away as the North Riding of Yorkshire, more than a hundred miles south of the border. With trouble brewing once more within England, the regency government decided that it could do without a war on two fronts. In October 1327 Isabella and Mortimer opened negotiations with King Robert, fully prepared to give the Scots what they wanted. On 17 March 1328, the treaty was ratified in Edinburgh; on 4 May it was given final approval by Edward III's government in Northampton.

Perhaps not surprisingly, considering what was at stake, Bruce was prepared to be generous. In return for an acknowledgement that he and his heirs should be free to enjoy the kingdom of Scotland without having to pay homage for it, the Scottish king agreed to hand over £20,000, no doubt paid for largely by the tribute from northern England which had long swelled King Robert's coffers (though if the English had agreed to Harclay's treaty of 1324, Bruce would have been prepared to pay 40,000 marks or nearly £27,000). It was also agreed that David Bruce should marry Edward III's little sister, Joan – not least in order to prevent King Robert from looking for a French bride for his son – and that both kingdoms would provide military aid to each other, except against France, with whom Scotland had been formally allied since 1326. Edward III was also obliged to use his influence with the pope to have the sentence of excommunication on Scotland repealed – a clause that he successfully discharged before the end of the year.

King Robert next proposed to deal with the trickiest issue of all; namely how the claims of what became known as the Disinherited should be treated. These were the men and women in both kingdoms who had lost lands by taking one side or the other during the war. Bruce aimed to keep things simple: no one was to be restored to their lands and tenements in the other kingdom. In practice, the pressure on the English government from men like Henry Beaumont, who claimed the Earldom of Buchan, was too intense and the final treaty made no mention of the Disinherited. This was to prove disastrous in the long run, though it is entirely understandable that such a contentious issue was not allowed to disrupt the peace process in 1327–28.

On 12 July 1328, Prince David and Princess Joan were married in Berwick Castle, which had received a spruce up that included new windows. Earl Thomas Randolph and Sir James Douglas were appointed to organise the feast, which cost over £1,500. Sufficient wine was provided and drunk to bring the wedding guests to such a pitch of excitement that they managed to knock down a churchyard wall.[62] The bride was accompanied by her mother, Isabella, and Mortimer, but the two kings were conspicuous by their absence.

Bruce claimed an indisposition that, however believable, was also likely to have been diplomatic. Edward III, outraged that his government should have agreed to a final peace at a time when it was well known that the Scottish king had little time to live, refused to attend. His feelings were echoed by the London mob, which prevented the Stone of Scone from being removed from Westminster Abbey as the peace treaty had promised. It lay there for another 668 years, until it was returned on loan to Scotland in 1996 by John Major's Conservative government.

King Robert's indisposition was certainly not sufficient to prevent him from going to Ireland within a month of his son's nuptials. Intent on securing the western approaches to his kingdom, he took with him his nephew, William de Burgh, to be installed as Earl in Ulster. In truth, the Anglo-Norman wedge represented by the de Burghs, dividing the native Irish from each other, did not last long, for Earl William was murdered only five years later in 1333. But King Robert would not know that.

At last it was time for some well-earned rest. Since 1326 Bruce had been building a manor house at Cardross, his dislike of castles applying to himself as much as everyone else. It lay near Dumbarton (see Map) and the River Clyde, whose waters – tidal until this point – allowed easy access by galley out into the Irish Sea and the bays and islands of the west coast beyond. The manor was set in parkland, presumably for hunting, though Bruce was perhaps only rarely in any condition to enjoy it. James Douglas had his own bedroom there and, for the first half of 1329, seems to have been in almost constant attendance on the king.

By May, Bruce knew that his death was imminent and made arrangements for what should become of his mortal remains. He had long wished to go on crusade, perhaps to atone for his earlier sins, but just as likely because it was the goal of all diligent knights and he may well have heard tales of the great wonders of the Holy Land from his grandfather, Bruce the Competitor. He therefore ordered that, once he was dead, his heart should be removed and embalmed, ready for one final journey.

Robert the Bruce, erstwhile Earl of Carrick and Lord of Annandale, King of Scots for twenty-three years, died at Cardross on 7 June 1329. His body, minus its heart and entrails, was carried in a litter across the country to Dunfermline Abbey and interred in what had been the royal mausoleum for over two centuries. Finally, in death, lying among previous Kings of Scots, including his hero David I, Robert the Bruce gained the unimpeachable legitimacy which had eluded him in life. His tomb, constructed in Paris, was made of white marble covered in gold leaf and surrounded by intricate ironwork. The epitaph read:

> Here lies the unconquered Robert, blessed king
> Who reads his deeds lives again all the battles he fought.
> By probity he brought to freedom
> The kingdom of the Scots;
> Now he dwells in the Heaven's heights.

The day after the interment, Barbour writes, the company 'sad and sorry ... went [upon] their way'.[63] It is testament to the peaceful nature of the times that 5-year-old David Bruce was not immediately crowned king, presumably on account of his tender years.

Sir James Douglas left Scotland roughly a year later, carrying his former comrade-in-arms' heart in a silver casket. Though he originally intended to travel to the Holy

Land, he decided to stop off en route in southern Spain to join Alfonso XI in his campaign against the Moors of Granada. Sir James is reputed to have travelled in grand style, 'keeping royal estate', and arrived in August 1330 to join Alfonso at the siege of Teba, 70 miles north-west of Malaga. The Christian forces then engaged a Muslim relief force and it seems that Douglas misinterpreted the enemy's tactics, forging ahead to attack it in the belief that it was retreating when in fact it was not. It was a typically audacious strategy on the part of the Scottish knight, but he and his men were surrounded. Realising that this was to be his last battle, the Good Sir James reputedly flung the casket with King Robert's heart ahead of him and plunged into the fray. His men discovered his body, along with the casket, the following day, when the Muslims were defeated. Both were brought home to Scotland. Sir James was buried in his own church of Douglas, while Bruce's heart was finally laid to rest in Melrose Abbey.

Thomas Randolph survived only another two years, dying suddenly at Musselburgh on 20 July 1332. This, more than the death of the old king and the precipitate demise of James Douglas, was bad news indeed for Scotland, for the Guardian was in the middle of military preparations against the Disinherited. They now wasted no time in setting sail for Scotland, landing on the Fife coast on 6 August. Among them was Edward Balliol. Just over a month later, King John's son was crowned at Scone, having already performed homage to Edward III in secret. By May 1334, 10-year-old King David and his queen had been sent to safety in France. The war had begun again.

Thus the bitter conflict between England and Scotland, and between the Bruces and the Balliols, did not end in 1328. But that does not alter what King Robert achieved in his lifetime. Although his reputation has inevitably been mythologised and he must bear the responsibility for creating some of the problems he faced, Bruce's achievements are nonetheless very real and impressive. He is indisputably one of the greatest kings Scotland has ever known and towers above his contemporaries in the British Isles, and indeed much further afield, for his military skill and command. By taking on seemingly impossible odds and finding that it was in his power to overcome them, he stands not just as a giant in his own time, but for all time.

Notes

1   *The Ipsos-MORI Social Policy Monitor.*
2   See, for example, Wright, T. (ed.), *The Chronicle of Pierre de Langtoft*, Vol. 2 (Rolls Series, 1868), p. 366, line 20. This work ends with the death of Edward I in 1307 and therefore shows that Robert was known as 'the Bruce' during his lifetime.
3   A Guardian (or Guardians) ruled when the Scottish king could not.
4   The Competitor died in 1295.
5   Now a part of Ayrshire on the south-west coast of Scotland.
6   Fordun, John of, *Chronicle of the Scottish Nation*, Vol. 2, Skene, F.J.H. & W.F. (eds) (Edmonston and Douglas, 1872), pp. 289–90.
7   Barrow, G.W.S., *Robert Bruce and the Community of the Realm of Scotland* (Edinburgh University Press, 2005), p. 193.
8   Ibid., pp. 199 passim.
9   See Broun, D., 'A New Look at Gesta Annalia Attributed to John of Fordun', in *Church, Chronicle and Learning in Medieval and Early Renaissance Scotland* (Mercat, 1999).

10   *Robert Bruce and the Community*, op. cit., p. 189.

11   *Chronicle of the Scottish Nation*, op. cit., p. 180. See Watson, F., *Macbeth: A True History* (Quercus, 2010), chapter 10.

12   *The Chronicle of Walter of Hemingburgh*, Vol. 2 (English Historical Society, 1849), p. 250.

13   Barbour, John, *The Bruce* (Canongate, 1997), p. 91.

14   As in hobgoblin. With thanks to Dr Robert Jones.

15   *The Bruce*, op. cit., p. 296ff.

16   Ibid., p. 64.

17   Ibid., pp. 332–5.

18   *Robert Bruce and the Community*, op. cit., pp. 228, 230.

19   *The Records of the Parliaments of Scotland to 1707* (*RPS*), 2007–2013, 1309/1; *The Bruce*, op. cit., p. 189 note 188.

20   *RPS*, ibid., 1309/2.

21   See Lynch, M., *Scotland: A New History* (Pimlico, 1993), p. 100.

22   See http://britishlibrary.typepad.co.uk/ digitisedmanuscripts/2013/06/robert-the-bruce- letter-found-at-british-library.html for a translation of this letter.

23   The English kings were also Dukes of Gascony.

24   McNamee, Colm, *The Wars of the Bruces* (Tuckwell Press, 1997), p. 251.

25   This Treaty of Inverness revived the Treaty of Perth (1266), whereby Norway ceded the Western Isles to Scotland for a lump sum and an annual payment.

26 *Calendar of Documents relating to Scotland* (CDS),
    Vol. 2, 1884, No. 1510.

27 Maxwell, H. (ed.), *Chronicle of Lanercost* (James
    Maclehose & Sons, 1913), pp. 201–2.

28 *The Bruce*, op. cit., pp. 336–43. The ladders used at
    Perth were still plain wooden ones.

29 See ibid., p. 338ff for a discussion of the discrepancy
    between the sources.

30 Ibid., pp. 368ff. This may be an apocryphal tale.

31 Ibid., pp. 374, 386ff. Unlike Bruce and Douglas,
    Randolph (and Edward Bruce) had no important
    descendants to flatter when Barbour was writing.

32 Smith, Alexander, *A Summer in Skye* (Strahan, 1866).

33 Barbour incorrectly states that Edward Bruce
    agreed this in June 1313, supposedly to his brother's
    annoyance: *The Bruce*, op. cit., p. 406.

34 Hunting reserves would be wooded but not densely,
    so that horsemen could chase their prey.

35 *The Bruce*, op. cit., pp. 462–4.

36 Ibid., p. 462.

37 Non-combatants or perhaps late arrivals whom
    Bruce would not allow into his well-drilled
    schiltroms.

38 *The Bruce*, op. cit., p. 462.

39 Denholm-Young, N. (ed.), *Vita Edwardi Secundi*
    (Thomas Nelson & Sons, 1957), p. 56.

40 Holmes, Richard, 'Cavalry', in *The Oxford
    Companion to Military History* (Oxford University
    Press, 2001), p. 187.

41 *The Bruce*, op. cit., p. 458.

42 Ibid., pp. 458, 460. This speech appears in a source contemporary to Bannockburn and so can be considered genuine.

43 Viard, J. & Déprez, E., *Chronique de Jean le Bel*, Vol. 1 (Paris, 1904), pp. 5–6, 85.

44 *RPS*, op. cit., 1315/1.

45 *Chronicle of the Scottish Nation*, op. cit., p. 340.

46 CDS, op. cit., Vol. 3, No. 473.

47 The most obvious example of this is Barbour's claim that Edward Bruce made a surrender agreement with Stirling Castle a whole year before the Battle of Bannockburn, thus prompting Edward of England to gather an army and come north. This was quite untrue.

48 *Wars of the Bruces*, op. cit., p. 74.

49 RPS, op. cit., 1318/24.

50 Beam, Amanda, *The Balliol Dynasty, 1264–1364* (John Donald, 2008), chapters 7, 8, p. 197. The vast Balliol lands in England and Scotland no longer belonged to the family.

51 http://www.nas.gov.uk/downloads/declarationArbroath.pdf.

52 Penman, M., 'A fell coniuracioun agayn Robert the douchty king: the Soules conspiracy of 1318–1320', in *Innes Review*, Vol. 50, Issue 1, 1999.

53 *The Bruce*, op. cit., p. 702.

54 *Lanercost*, op. cit., p. 232.

55 Väthjunker, S., 'A Study of the Career of Sir James Douglas: The Historical Record Versus Barbour's Bruce' (Unpublished thesis, University of Aberdeen, 1992), pp. 100–2.

56 Brown, Michael, *The Wars of Scotland, 1214–1371* (Edinburgh University Press, 2004), p. 222.

57 RPS, op. cit., 1328/1.

58 Phillips, Seymour, *Edward II* (Yale University Press, 2010), pp. 546–7.

59 *Wars of the Bruces*, op. cit., pp. 242–5.

60 *Lanercost*, op. cit., p. 257.

61 'Career of Sir James Douglas', op. cit., pp. 111–5; *The Bruce*, op. cit., p. 777.

62 *The Bruce*, ibid., p. 744, note 72.

63 *The Bruce*, op. cit., p. 756, including note 303.

Timeline

1274	Birth of Robert Bruce
1286	Death of Alexander III
1289	Treaty of Salisbury (prelude to marriage of Maid of Norway to Prince Edward)
1290	Death of Maid of Norway
1291–92	The Great Cause (court presided over by Edward I to choose new King of Scots)
1292	John Balliol chosen as king
1296	King Edward invades Scotland and deposes King John
1297	Uprisings all over Scotland, including one led by the Earl of Carrick
	September: Battle of Stirling Bridge
1298	July: William Wallace defeated by Edward I at Battle of Falkirk
	Earl of Carrick and John Comyn, the younger, of Badenoch become Guardians
1300	Carrick ousted as Guardian by the Comyns
1302	Carrick accepts King Edward as his overlord when it looks likely that King John will be returning with a French army

1304	General submissions of Scots to Edward I; Carrick is made Sheriff of Lanark and Ayr 21 April: Death of Carrick's father Agreement of mutual aid made between Carrick and Bishop William Lamberton
1306	Carrick murders John Comyn of Badenoch 25 March: Carrick is made king Carrick is defeated at Methven and flees west
1307	King Robert returns to mainland Scotland and adopts successful guerrilla tactics 7 July: Death of Edward I
1308	Defeat of John Comyn of Buchan at Inverurie; sends Comyn faction into exile
1309	March: King Robert holds his first parliament at St Andrews Letters sent by nobles and clergy to King of France justifying Bruce's kingship
1310	Edward II manages to campaign in Scotland
1311	Scoto-Norwegian treaty agreed; raids on northern England begin
1313	October: Ultimatum issued giving Scottish landowners one year to accept Bruce as king
1314	Battle of Bannockburn; most Scottish landowners submit to King Robert
1315	Return of Bruce's women; siege of Carlisle; Edward Bruce begins campaigning in Ireland
1318	October: Edward Bruce killed in Ireland Capture of Berwick by the Scots

1320	Declaration of Arbroath sent to try to persuade the pope not to excommunicate Scotland; plot to replace Bruce with Edward Balliol
1323	Thirteen-year truce agreed between Scotland and England
1324	5 March: Birth of David Bruce
1326	Civil war in England
1327	20 January: Deposition of Edward II 21 September: King Edward II dies at Berkeley Castle Scots invade England
1328	Treaty of Northampton-Edinburgh brings an end to the war
1329	7 June: Death of King Robert I at Cardross

Further Reading

Barbour, John, *The Bruce* (Canongate, 2007)

Barrow, G.W.S., *Robert Bruce and the Community of the Realm of Scotland* (Edinburgh University Press, 2005)

Beam, Amanda, *The Balliol Dynasty, 1264–1364* (John Donald, 2008)

Brown, Chris, *Bannockburn 1314: A New History* (The History Press, 2009)

Brown, Michael, *The Wars of Scotland, 1214–1371* (Edinburgh University Press, 2004)

Brown, Michael, *Bannockburn: The Scottish War and the British Isles, 1307–1323* (Edinburgh University Press, 2008)

Frame, Robin, *The Political Development of the British Isles, 1100–1400* (Clarendon Press, 1995)

Houston, R.A. & Knox, B., *The Penguin History of Scotland* (Penguin, 2002)

McNamee, Colm, *The Wars of the Bruces* (Tuckwell Press, 1997)

McNamee, Colm, *Robert Bruce: Our Most Valiant Prince, King and Lord* (Birlinn, 2006)

Phillips, Seymour, *Edward II* (Yale University Press, 2011)

Prestwich, Michael, *Edward I* (Yale University Press, 2007)

Watson, Fiona, *Under the Hammer: Edward I and Scotland* (John Donald, 2009)

Young, Alan, *Robert the Bruce's Rivals: The Comyns, 1212– 1314* (Tuckwell Press, 1997)

Web Links

There are a number of websites dedicated to Robert the Bruce. Some of them should be treated with caution. The following are the most helpful. Many of these are designed for schools, but provide a good overview and resources.

http://www.breakingofbritain.ac.uk/schools
http://www.educationscotland.gov.uk/
   higherscottishhistory/warsofindependence/index.asp
http://www.educationscotland.gov.uk/scotlandshistory/
   warsofindependence/robertbruce/index.asp
http://www.bbc.co.uk/scotland/history/wars_of_
   independence
http://www.stirlingcastle.gov.uk/inv-wars-of-
   independence.pdf
http://www.scottisharchivesforschools.org/
   WarsOfIndependence/Index.asp
http://edwardthesecond.blogspot.co.uk – Everything
   you ever wanted to know about Edward II, properly
   researched
http://www.historvius.com/wars-of-scottish-
   independence-sites/pe168 – A guide to key sites from
   the period

Acknowledgements

I am most grateful to Tony Morris for commissioning this book and giving Robert Bruce the recognition he deserves.

Giuseppe **Verdi** Henry V **Brunel** Pope John Paul II **Jane Austen** William the Conqueror **Abraham Lincoln** Robert the Bruce **Charles Darwin** Buddha **Elizabeth I** Horatio Nelson **Wellington** Hannibal & Scipio **Jesus** Joan of Arc **Anne Frank** Alfred the Great **King Arthur** Henry Ford **Nelson Mandela**